Scholarly Principles in Teacher Education

Waxmann Verlag GmbH
Steinfurter Straße 555, 48159 Münster
info@waxmann.com

European Studies on Educational Practices

Edited by
Anna Herbert and Anja Kraus

Volume 6

Editorial Board

Nanna Lueth, Berlin/Germany
Carol Taylor, Sheffield/England
Tatiana Shchyttsova, Vilnius/Lithuania
Fatma Saçlı, Nevşehir/Turkey

Educational practices comprise intentions, movements, bodies, language, things and spaces. Our aim in this series is to develop theoretical perspectives, and combine them with empirical approaches in order to create a scientific forum for interdisciplinary perspectives on educational practices, experiences and their contexts. The interpretative approach of this book series entails theoretical, political, esthetical, methodological and methodical questions. By taking a European perspective, it becomes apparent that the theoretical and practical understanding of pedagogical terms framing educational practices like education, didactics, methods etc. differs very much from one language area and culture of interpretation to another. We regard this as an expression of cultural diversity and want to promote communication about the similarities and differences within the international field of research.

The book series "European Studies on Educational Practices" constitutes an international forum to make theoretical and empirical approaches to pedagogical practices noticeable and thus available to a wide audience. Publications are mainly in English, but in German or Swedish, as well.

The main aim is to establish a view on education as a field of practices, directed by plannings, designs, social relations and structures, privileges, values and outcomes. Our view on practices stems from taking the manifold and often tacit dimensions of pedagogy into account. By taking an interdisciplinary approach, the book series will open up new insights into educational practices and art forms, into the relation between theory and practice, and into the aims and purposes of education. Our hope is to investigate and challenge pedagogy as central to reflexivity and life skills.

Anja Kraus

Scholarly Principles in Teacher Education

What Kind of Science Serves a Practice-Oriented Teacher Education?

Waxmann 2015
Münster • New York

The publication is supported by a contribution
from Linnaeus University, Sweden

Bibliographic information published by the Deutsche Nationalbibliothek
The Deutsche Nationalbibliothek lists this publication in the
Deutsche Nationalbibliografie; detailed bibliographic data
are available in the Internet at http://dnb.d-nb.de

European Studies on Educational Practices, Volume 6

ISSN 2193-7141
ISBN 978-3-8309-3264-2
Ebook-ISBN 978-3-8309-8264-5

© Waxmann Verlag GmbH, 2015
Münster, Germany

www.waxmann.com
info@waxmann.com

Cover Design: Anne Breitenbach, Münster
Typesetting: Sven Solterbeck, Münster

Printed on age-resistant paper,
acid-free according to ISO 9706

Printed in Germany

All rights reserved. No part of this publication may be reproduced, stored
in a retrieval system or transmitted in any form or by any means, electronic,
electrostatic, magnetic tape, mechanical, photocopying, recording or
otherwise without permission in writing from the copyright holder.

Contents

Introduction.. 7

1.	Current Controversies on Teacher Education................	11
1.1	The Aims of the Council of the European Union............	11
1.2	Current Controversies about Teacher Education and its Historical Background	12
1.3	The Relation of Theory and Practice in Professional Teaching and its Relation to Scientific Approaches......................	32
1.3.1	Practical Knowledge and the Orientation of Teachers in Comparison with Scientific Approaches...................	34
2.	The Challenge of a Relation of the General and the Particular in Scientific Thinking and Research...........................	54
2.1	The Phenomenological Noematic and the Noetic Concept of Science as a Basis for Modeling Teacher Education.........	60
2.2	On the Noematic Concept of Science.......................	63
2.2.1	Criticism of Noematic Models of Teacher Education	65
2.2.1.1	Teacher Education as a Development of "Competences"	66
2.2.1.2	Standards, Standardized Teaching and Teacher Education.....	69
2.2.1.3	Teacher Education as a Development of "Subjective Theories" and the Concept of "Reflective Practitioning"................	70
2.2.1.4	Criticism of the Noematic Concept of Science in Education and Outlook on the Phenomenological Noetic Alternative	73
2.3	On the Phenomenological Noetic Concept of Science.........	81
2.3.1	Knowledge Forms and Knowledge Formats	85
2.3.2	"Epistemology"	87
3.	Science from the Phenomenological Noetic Perspective.......	89
3.1	On Phenomenological Epistemology.......................	91
3.1.1	Body-Phenomenology and the Concept of a "Constitutive Corporality"	92
3.1.2	On Body-Phenomenological Epistemology.................	95
3.2	On Performativity-Oriented Epistemology..................	98
3.3	On Praxeological Epistemology...........................	107

4.	The Epistemology of Science-Oriented Teacher Education and Empirical Approaches to Orientative and Practical Knowledge of Teachers	110
4.1	The Practice Knowledge and Orientation Knowledge of Teachers in the Classroom from the Phenomenological Noetic Perspective	112

References. 122

*"[A] culture of the senses, that is in the end:
the development of judgment."*[1]

Introduction

The question what kind of teaching fits to the life-world(s) of the pupils and is as well oriented at their future prospects has always formed the center of Curriculum Studies as an important reference science of teacher education.[2] Today, both objectives of teaching are put together in the aim of developing competences, specified as the attainment of practical knowledge.

Today, all forms of formal and informal learning, also professional formation, and especially teacher education[3], are interpreted as a development of competences. The interpretation of the relationship of theory, research, and (everyday as well as specialized) practices plays a central role in conceptualizing the development of competences. There is a public as well as a scientific debate about the different interpretations of this relationship. The differences that are brought up in this context correspond with the different concepts of science.

---

1 GADAMER 1979, p. 23, transl. by A.K. GADAMER (1979) links the development of judgement with that of common sense ("sensus communis") and describes judgement as a capacity to subsume "[…] a *particular under a universal, recognising something* as an *example* of a *rule*" (GADAMER [1993] 2001, p. 31), "[…] because no demonstration from concepts is able to guide the application of rules", rather judgement can only be "practised from case to case".
2 There is great diversity in teacher education systems and approaches to learning and teaching practice across Europe (and within the German states), even though the practical everyday problems of the various education systems are rather similar. In the field of research on Didactics, here University Didactics for teacher education, one progressively realizes that it is important to overcome fragmentation and to find common ground. (Cf. HUDSON & MEYER 2011)
3 In the German context: "Lehrerbildung". Bildung (German for "education" and "formation") refers to the tradition of self-education as a process of personal, social and cultural formation (cf. VON HUMBOLDT [1836] 1999). "Bildung" refers to a process as well as a state of mind. It is the mainly personal process of shaping one's own humanity as well as one's innate intellectual skills in terms of taking over social responsibility. "Bildung" refers to the ideal of a reflexivity that is directed to oneself, to others and to the world. Philosophy and education are linked in a manner that thus refers to a process of personal as well as cultural maturation.

This essay concentrates on the question of how to model a practically, and at the same time scientifically oriented teacher education. At first some of the current models of teacher education are discussed in terms of their science-theoretical background.[4] Specifically, the relationship of theory or research and (everyday) practice in teacher education will be reflected epistemologically. From this view a concept of sciences will be developed that promises to give hints at an academic teacher education oriented at the professional practices of a teacher as well as at science that are relevant for teaching: the so called "noetic" concept of science. The noetic concept of science also makes it possible to keep distance from "grand narratives", like "progress", "Enlightenment", "emancipation", defined by Francois LYOTARD [1979] 1984 as an effort by ruling elites to explain how the status quo had evolved and, in the process, to rationalize why the status quo was destined to emerge and needed to be embraced.[5]

Education, in the German tradition the "grand narrative" of "Bildung", describes the process of becoming self-determining as well as socially responsible in judgement and acting. In terms of a classroom practice education cannot be separated from diverse normative factors or from didactics as the theory and practice of teaching and learning.

The main professional task of a teacher is to set processes of learning and education in motion. This task is focused in this essay. Aspects of the development of subject-related, or other competences that are not directly connected to teaching will not be taken into consideration. More precisely, the focus of this essay is on the formally framed development of such skills and abilities that are important in terms of grasping and using the specifics of an educational situation in order to influence the learning conditions at hand, with the aim to initiate processes of learning and education.[6]

We will argue: There is no uniform theory of the teaching profession, because the diverse and complex pedagogical realities as a professional reality can hardly be represented by the linearity and strong coherence of theoretical knowledge. Moreover, one meets a variety of professional practices, which allow for different

---

4   Cf. KRON 1999
5   The "noetic" concept of sciences (cf. DIEMER 1964) is not to be confused with "noetic sciences", represented e.g. by the Institute of Noetic Sciences in Petaluma, as there is neither a reference to any kind of "mystery of human consciousness", nor to "healing, extended human capacities and worldview transformation" (see: http://www.noetic.org/about/overview/).
6   Presumably, the contexts of a formally framed initializing, structuring and assessment of learning can be, in a modified form, transferred to other task areas of the teaching profession.

interpretations and which influence the self-understanding and the acting of the professionals in various ways. Therefore, the result of many empirical studies is not surprising that a complex theoretical knowledge is reduced to specific (professional) situations in the pedagogical field, in which theoretical knowledge appears to be fragmentary and sporadic. Teaching primarily presupposes the abilities to perceive, to understand and to reflect the capabilities of the pupils in a classroom, and to take professional decisions. These proficiencies can be most likely defined as the ability to act appropriately in each individual case. This means taking the factors into account that are relevant for the understanding of a situation at hand, such as e.g. the action objectives and the heteromorph normative orientations of the acting individuals, as well as the intra-, interpersonal, or intercultural tensions arising among them.

According to the phenomenological noetic approach the origin of knowledge and insight, of scientific concepts and results as well as their application are based on social and cultural conditions, relationships and practices. Therefore, science is not free from normative implications.[7] In consequence, the fundamental question "[…] about the significance of [scientific] insights in terms of virulent epistemological, poietical and practical-ethical problems"[8] is in the focus of scientific research. The phenomenological noetic approach, and this is the main hypothesis of this essay, opens up the possibility not only to analyze the professional reflexivity in terms of educational and teaching practices, but also to develop it within teacher education. It reflects the fact that educational and teaching practices are determined by diverse, not only cognitive forms and formats of knowledge.[9] Out of the phenomenological noetic perspective, thus, the widespread limitation of the scientific orientation to rational, merely textual and metrical models of explanation and knowledge is confronted with another form of thinking that is open to manifold forms and formats of knowledge. Noetic scientific approaches can thus be regarded as suitable for investigating as well as for structuring and also for developing the reflexivity fitting for the professional field in question.

The scientific background of a science- as well as practically oriented teacher education is thus more closely defined as and specified by the noetic perspective. In this essay, we step forward to the modeling of a pedagogical quality development of academic teaching in the field of teacher education as well as to a science

---

7   Cf. MANNHEIM 1936, LONGINO 2001, etc.
8   RHEIN 2010, p. 46, transl. by A.K.
9   Cf. SCHÖN 1983

research[10] and university research[11] from the perspective of Educational Sciences. In a spiral argumentation the hypothesis of a noetic approach to a practically-oriented and scientific teacher education is deepened step by step.

As this essay was originally written in German[12], there is a special need for working on terms which are used in the German-speaking professional community.

Anja Kraus, Växjö in March 2015

---

10 HUG (1996) in detail refers to this desideratum.
11 GROPPE (2014) lately referred to this desideratum.
12 KRAUS (2015).

1. Current Controversies on Teacher Education

1.1 The Aims of the Council of the European Union

The agreement on the objectives for teacher education which were approved by the Council of the European Union in October 2007 in Brussels define the profile of competences of teachers with the focus on social change resulting from diverse processes of modernization.[13] The program of "lifelong learning" forms the center of the current controversies about the question what is relevant to societies today, as seen from an economic, political and social perspective. This program is spelled out as the idea of a continuing professionalization, respectively a competence development. The professional profile of a teacher is diversified in subject-specific and methodical, social and personal competences. Besides that, in the agreement on the objectives for teacher education by the Council of the European Union cultural diversity plays a major role. Beside the willingness and ability to cooperate with colleagues, parents and with non-school organizations, competences that are connected to mobility and the task area of a quality assurance are further important facets of the spectrum of professional competences that is allotted to be developed in the frame of ("life-long") teacher education.[14]

The European contract focuses on the interlinkage of altogether three phases of teacher education: After the academic studies a so called "early career support" shall follow, which merges into a "mutual monitoring support" to be perchance enriched by experiences abroad. In terms of the second phase, experiences are stressed that are made in one's own as well as in other professional fields. These experiences are, according to the "European Qualifications Framework for Lifelong Learning"[15], of central importance already in the first phase of the academic teacher education. The regular exercise of the profession is seen as the third phase of qualification.

In the agreement on the objectives for teacher education by the Council of the European Union the balance of theory and praxis plays a central role in the sense of reflected educational and teaching practices on one hand, and as an innovative development of knowledge in the frame of the professional activity on the other hand. This twofold task involves the task of building up a relationship between the

---

13   A survey on the manifold European political initiatives see: FREDRIKSSON & HOSKINS 2007 and FREDRIKSSON 2006.
14   Cf. EUROPEAN COMMISSION 2008
15   Cf. EUROPEAN COMMISSION 2008

educational practices in school, and science. This relationship is the topic of this essay.

In the following, at first current concepts of a science- as well as practically oriented teacher education will be sketched out. Starting from a critique of these concepts, an alternative understanding will be unfolded.

1.2 Current Controversies about Teacher Education and its Historical Background

In the diverse concepts of the theory-praxis relationship in teaching the question of the role of a profession-related science for teacher education is addressed differently. Teacher education is thus a kind of *colored dog* regarding its references to science. In the first hand it is a topic of Educational Sciences and its disciplines, specifically of the (curriculum-, organization- or profession-theoretical) research on Didactics, the Curriculum Studies[16], and, besides that, Educational Psychology and research on Subject Didactics (this does not imply any claim to completeness). Also sociological, philosophical and cultural scientific approaches play an important role in modeling teacher education at the university. Transverse to these very different disciplines are Curriculum Research, School and Classroom Research, Teacher Education Research, Teacher Research, research on professional development and Pupil Research with their analyses of teaching and learning in the classroom. In thematic and/or methodical regards these research directions have, to a greater or a less extent, diverse liaisons with the before-mentioned disciplines. The same is true for the quantitative empirical research on teaching and learning and for a research on school effectiveness that works with the paradigms of an "excellent teacher", a "good school" etc. Nowadays, also socio-economic and governmental models play a central role for the modeling of teacher education.

However, in principle the issue of the professional knowledge in the field of teaching is linked to the historical images (a) of the "teacher"[17] and (b) of the "pupil". The images of the central acting persons correspond with the different and changing ideas of teaching (c). These images are fundamental to the practices of teaching, respectively to the lesson planning, to the reflection and (re-)construc-

---

16 In German: Schulpädagogik, (literally pedagogy in school) also research on Didactics, is a scientific discipline in European, except for the English-speaking countries. While lesson planning and class management are the central subjects of Curriculum Studies, research on Didactics is moreover a reading of learning and teaching as a pedagogical relation aiming at "Bildung" (see above). (Cf. HUDSON & MEYER 2011)

17 Cf. MAYR & NEUWEG 2006

tion of situations of teaching and learning, as well as to the scientific research on them. Therefore, these images are key factors in the models of a scientific teacher education (d).

(a) Images of the teacher:

The assumption that the teacher personality is a set of relatively stable dispositions that are innate and crucial for professional acting is historically of major importance. However, it is also at times put in question.[18] The so called "personality paradigm" corresponds with the historical fact that teacher education, except for (subject-oriented) programs for high school teaching, worldwide only recently found a place in the universities. Research on teacher education has always, first as a historical side path, been convinced of the possibility to develop professionality in a formal educational frame. In the 1970ies, and reinforced since the turn of the millennium, and in the course of an increasing scientification of teacher education the paradigm of personality has been confronted with the so called "process-product-paradigm". According to this paradigm one focuses on governable abilities of teaching. Since the 1980ies and according to the so called "cognitive turn" the development of psychometrically modeled and empirically reasonable competences is in the center of public as well as of specialist discussion. Competences are meant to be measurable as an output[19] of learning and they correspond to the so called "expert paradigm". One can read the "expert paradigm" as a kind of new edition of

---

18 Cf. MAYR & NEUWEG 2006
19 Governmental theories of quality development of school and teaching make a differentiation between an "input-control", in which a teacher and her/his teaching are in the forground, and an "output-control" of the learning results or of the students' evaluation of their learning. For an output-control standardised tests and the anonymous external evaluation is in the center of the quality development of school and teaching. The terms input- and output-control serve e.g. as the criteria for the ways to applicate the national curricula. These ways are discussed controversially in the field of Educational Sciences. Here a statement of Wilfried Bos et al. (2007, p. 1, transl. by A.K.) shall be representative for those positions which are not shared in this treatise: "The experiences in other countries, which regularly give a very good performance in the international pupil assessment studies (e.g. Canada, England, Finland, the Netherlands and Sweden), show that a regular 'output control' long- and medium-term positively influence the competence development of the pupils." Scientific research for Sweden, in contrary, shows that there are no clear effect relations between 'output control' and the achievements of the students in school; neither is there a pronounced tradition of 'output control'. (Cf. SKOLVERKET 2009)

the "personality paradigm".[20] This is also true for other models, which are oriented at the "output" of education as well as at the "best practice" research, such as e.g. the "excellent teacher" concept. Johannes MAYR & Georg Hans NEUWEG (2006) point out the premises of this revival: "With the approach of a *personality reflexive* [accentuation by J.M. & G.H.N.] teacher education one becomes aware of how important it is to widen the reflection, additionally to a research-oriented, cognitively accentuated and outward facing reflection, to inward processes and to make one's own experiences in situations of interaction the object of observation."[21] Today – also in terms of the wide range of diverse descriptions of the role of a teacher (coach, guide etc.) – the consideration is dominant that such a (not in any case science-based) self-reflection, which is supposed to be oriented at given professional ethics, is measurable as standards[22]. Latterly, such standards are brought to the foreground in nearly all the phases of teacher education (beginning with orientation tests for potential teacher students). However, the "expert paradigm" is criticized because of ignoring and attenuating the aspects of the (teacher) profession that cannot easily be called into consciousness as they are not articulable and not measurable. In this essay an alternative approach shall be offered.

(b)   Images of the pupil:

An active understanding of the role of a distinctive (and innate) teacher personality corresponds to the image of pupils as externally more or less passive, mostly receptively acting educandi. Scientifically, pupils are mostly investigated in this

---

20   Cf. MAYR & NEUWEG 2006, DAHLBERG et al. 2002
21   MAYR & NEUWEG 2006, p. 198, transl. by A.K.
22   In "Standards for Teacher Education of the Secretary of the Standing Conference of the State Ministers of Education and the Arts in the Federal Republic of Germany" (KMK 2004, transl. by A.K.) "standards" are defined as follows: "The term 'standard' frequently produces misunderstandings in the contexts of education and vocational training, because it is not used in a standardised way. According to its meaning a standard is a demarcation of the desirable characteristics of an object or a process in terms of well-defined quality criteria, which are as precise as possible. By formulating a standard one decides 'what is standard'. That such a standard has a general validity and everybody accepts there its high degree of reliability in terms of describing an object or process. This reliability is a precondition for the application and use of the objects or processes 'standardised' in this way in different contexts in terms of their purpose without any problems; all the other elements of a specific context can expect the equivalence of the deployed element with the general standards to which they apply."

sense, respectively as the objects of education.[23] This rather customary approach to educative processes is confronted by school practical approaches, as e.g. those that are oriented at the principle of "pupil orientation". In the 1920ies, "child-oriented" reform-pedagogical settings were developed, and in the 1970ies, the significance of socialization was put in the foreground of the dispositive "pupil". While the first was founded in trusting the good of the child and in optimism about education, the latter was linked to optimism about governance that at this time was meant in terms of promoting equal opportunities and emancipation. Pupils were encouraged to self-determination and participation, which should be supported by appropriate institutions and processes. Today the competent learner as the subject of self-organized and life-long learning is highlighted. Individual abilities and competences are modeled psychometrically.[24] However, since the 1990s specifically the action perspectives of the pupils and their views of themselves and the world are focused by the evolving Children's Studies[25] and Pupil

---

23 Cf. HACKL 2008
24 Cf. the Priority Program (SPP) 1293 of the German Research Foundation (DFG) that started in June 2006 and ended in 2010 is described as follows, transl. by A.K.: "The SPP is concerned with the foundations of the modelling of competences in Educational Sciences, Subject Didactics and Cognition Psychology as well as with psychometric models and concrete technologies to measure competences. For the SPP competences are defined as context-specific cognitive dispositions for effort-making [in German: Leistungsdisposition, mostly used in economics in the sense of activity scheduling], which in a functional way refer to situations and affordances of particular domains in the sense of specific areas of learning and acting. Competences are attained by making experiences and they can be influenced by institutionalised processes of education."
25 For the English-speaking realm see BOWMAN 2007. The idea of the interdisciplinary field of Children's Studies (which came up at Brooklyn College of The City University of New York in 1991) was the Human Rights of children. Thus, from its beginnings within Children's Studies the ontological claim was made that children must be viewed in their fullness as human beings and as a generational and social class in all its civic, political, social, economic and cultural dimensions. This field of reseach thus regards itself as an approach to the perspectives of children and youth from 0–18 years as "acting persons", across diverse academic disciplines. Children's Studies were coined in contradistinction to the Child Study Movement initiated by Stanley HALL at the turn of the 20th Century with its focus on Child Psychology and Developmental Psychology. Within Children's Studies in methodological regards the research *on* children has been in parts replaced by a research *with* children (cf. CHRISTENSEN & JAMES 2008). The research *with* children works out their perceptions, perspectives and views of reality by taking the social and material circumstances of their interpretative activities into account. The central and challenging task of the so called Children's Studies is posed by the claim that children must be viewed in their fullness as human

Research[26]. Their results and concepts merged into didactical considerations as well as into diverse fields of research on education. In the framework of recent Children's Studies and Pupil Research Georg BREIDENSTEIN & Kerstin JERGUS (2005) published e.g. the result, that pupils insist on a difference between them as a pupil and as a private person, and that they are even ready to defend this difference against opposition. In turn, they suggest paying attention primarily scientifically to the modes of the constitution of the role of the pupil in its significance for modeling the situation of teaching and formal learning. In this essay it is

---

beings and as well as a generational and social class in all its social, civic, political, economic and cultural dimensions. The main effort of Children's Studies is to pave the way for minors to express themselves. Its theoretical, methodological and methodical approaches consequently promise to support the conceptualization of participative pedagogical approaches of any kind. For the english-speaking context see JAMES & JAMES 2008 and LENZER 2001; see also Du BOIS-REYMOND et al. 2001. Today we find Childhood Studies, Children's Studies and Child Psychology programs at numerous academic institutions and worldwide. Whereas until now in Germany "a child" and "a pupil" is seen as a pertinent social identity in most of the theories on pedagogy and school (cf. HACKL 2008), already since the 1960s, stronger since the 1980ies, the sociologically-oriented Childhood Studies (referring to ARIÈS 1962, DE MAUSE 1974) have accepted that childhood is subject to a dramatic change within the course of time. They understand childhood as a construct; the prevalent objects of Childhood Studies are the causes as well as the issues of this construct. Describing the development of childhood in the previous decades (the 1950ies until the 1980ies) researchers spoke of a paradigmatic change, identifying it by the term "changed childhood". At the outset the "changed childhood" has mainly been discussed in terms of external factors such as e.g. prosperity, the influences of digital media, the increasing variety of family models, diverse phenomena of habitat fragmentation etc. Progressively, discovering also internal factors, such as e.g. the time management of pupils (ZEIHER 2001), or their experienced use of digital devices, the focus on socialisation shifted to that on individual self-regulation. At present, childhood is regarded as a social construct, and successively also the fact is recognized that children themselves interpret their own child-being (ROLFF & ZIMMERMANN 1993, p. 151 ff.). In the beginning of 1990ies thus the interdisciplinary field of Children's Studies was founded in terms of grasping a child's perspective on everyday civic, political, social, economic and cultural questions. With the comprehensive approach of study to the generational cohort of children from 0–18 years of age Childhood Studies as well as Children's Studies were introduced and coined in contradistinction to Child and Development Psychology. For the German-speaking context see: DECKERT-PEACEMAN et al. 2010 and HEINZEL 2000.

26 Pupil Research in the German-speaking field is comparable to the "Studies on Pupil Voice and Research" in the English-speaking realm.

argued that one should give more consideration to the insights of Pupil Research in modeling teacher education than it is actually the case.

(c)   Images of teaching and school:

The beginning of school is not defined, but it is most likely linked to the evidence of a writing culture (ca. 5300 b.C.). As one of the first, Wolfgang RATKE and John Amos COMENIUS in the 17th Century understood teaching and learning processes at school in terms of didactics and pedagogy. They looked at education as a pathway to become a human being by being introduced into the basic Christian beliefs and the Christian lifestyle. Besides that, education is regarded as the adequate means for changing society for the better; nowadays, the social and cultural tasks of school are still prevalent. However, already COMENIUS ([1657] 1896) criticized the school of its deficient relation to the concerns and practices of everyday life. This criticism is handed down as a basic motif in recent Western school history. In the first hand it was the reform pedagogical movement that considered this matter and developed counter-models for the school. Today, a standstill and a consolidation of the development of such reform pedagogical models are proven.[27] Wilhelm WITTENBRUCH (2010) refers this to an ethics of practicability that makes it difficult to follow pedagogical models in school practice. However, the traditional model for teaching and didactics, especially for the upper and lower secondary sections, is mainly oriented at the structures of the academic disciplines. In this respect teaching in school is usually understood as the transfer of specific logically and hierarchically structured inventories of knowledge. The mediated contents of learning are (in the best case) based on analysis and they are – sometimes more, in other cases less – didactically reduced[28]. For a decade, the degree to which the aims of learning and development in school are fulfilled has been surveyed in an increasing way by diverse quality control systems (cross-sectional and longitudinal studies, central testing systems etc.). The diverse concepts of a reform of school and teaching, however, operate since the time of Enlightment – and with different degrees of emphasis – with pedagogical and didactical principles. These principles are mostly directed to the learners. Along with an individualized view of the learners' ideas about learning concepts ruled by the orientation to activity and context play an important role. Increasingly, virtual learning environments are brought

---

27 E.g. WITTENBRUCH 2010; PETERSSEN 1996, p. 81 ff. or HERICKS & KUNZE 2004, p. 728
28 A "didactical reduction" or "didactical tranformation" as an important aspect of didactics is the filtering out of content from the complex whole of a theme in terms of a learner-centred instructive presentation. (Cf. HAUPTMEIER 1980)

into perspective. However, even in concepts of an instruction that is oriented at the pupils' learning being a pupil is almost seen as a mere complement of teaching.[29] In former and in actual didactics the pupils are thus typically identified with an abstraction; and this is often also true for classes in school.[30] Starting from this criticism, pedagogy and didactics are read not so much in terms of cognition and directing, but as implicit, corporally and socially mediated processes. Pedagogy is then regarded as oriented toward its personal, material and medial possibilities, and concepts to grasp these possibilities are brought up, such as the "hidden curriculum"[31] or the "frontstage"[32] of classes in contrast to their "backstage(s)". Actually, these concepts are worked out in critical, systemic, poststructuralistic and phenomenological analyses of pedagogical processes and models. This essay refers to these analyses.

(d)   Images of teacher education:

Teacher education has only recently entered the universities. Formerly it had its place at teacher academies. Moreover, at the universities the Higher Education Didactics, compared to other academic disciplines, tends to be given secondary treatment.

However, there is a deep-rooted educational mandate of the universities. German universities have been deeply influenced by Wilhelm von Humboldt's vision of "Bildung" as a process forming the characteristics of a person (in both

---

29   Hackl 2008, p. 78. Bernd Hackl argues that the idea of a prescriptive theory of teaching that is constitutive for didactics presupposes a masking of the real processes of teaching and learning and their interdependencies with items, structures and external events. He points at the desideratum of a scientific theory about the relationship between teaching and learning.
30   Hackl 2008
31   Jackson 1968; Zinnecker 1975
32   In the frame of School Research Jürgen Zinnecker (1978) refers to the theatre metaphor of Erving Goffman (1995) describing social relations and situations. He thus analyses processes of meaning-making in the frame of school in terms of the processes on the "frontstage" of a school lesson and its diverse "backstages". In lesson times the classroom is the "frontstage", while e.g. certain areas in the schoolyard are maybe used by the students as a "backstage". A "backstage" is a place for the students to work through their experiences in school as well as a place of grouping and of protest. Here, the students develop subcultures, and also mentally prepare for the teaching situation. As soon as the teacher leaves it, also the classroom can be transformed into a "backstage".

regards focused on the person) in terms of his/her self-education. Self-education, according to von Humboldt, is initiated by a type of education that is deeply linked with "cosmopolitanism". "Cosmopolitanism" is the ideology that all humans belong to a single community based on a shared morality. This morality is defined as follows: "[…] the ultimate task of our existence is to give the fullest possible content to the concept of humanity in our own person […] through the impact of actions in our own lives [… This task] can only be implemented through the links established between ourselves as individuals and the world around us."[33] The task of self-education is neither set by religious, nor by political authorities, nor by societal or economic affordances, but by the inner forces and potentials of each human being in an active engagement and in a "free" (based on Civic Rights) interaction with as many aspects of the world as possible. This kind of a general education for all citizens is connected to the mastery of language. von Humboldt's view shows thus an idealised and monocultural understanding of mankind. It can be seen within more and more apparent globalization processes raising the questions whether there is still space for educational concepts or ideals like emancipation, equal opportunities and fairness in distribution and democracy, or how these concepts have to be modified.[34]

However, since its foundation and partly until today, the interpretation of the mandate of the German university has been left up to the universities themselves, respectively to the academic teachers. In Germany, the "freedom of research and teaching" is a fundamental right.[35]

Seen from a historical point of view, teacher education has been critisized again and again of its deficitary practical relevance and even lack of foundation in reality. In the framework of the "student movement" in the early 1970s a fundamental critique of the academic teaching and of the study programs at universities led to diverse reforms, mainly directed to the organizational structures of universities. Student councils still complain that the key areas of teacher education programs, so to say the subject-oriented, subject-didactical and sociological disciplines are not sufficiently linked with the practical application in school, respectively the two learning areas are displayed side by side.[36] Since the 1980s there are empirically founded results of the surveys of student opinions.[37] For a long time criticism of

---

33 von Humboldt 1903–1920, p. 283, transl. by A.K.
34 Cf. Schröttner 2010
35 See Art. 5 (3) of the Basic Law for the Federal Republic of Germany: "Art and science, research and teaching are free".
36 Ulich 1996, p. 87
37 Cf. Stadelmann 2006, p. 14 f. About the problems of these assessments see Stadelmann 2006, p. 28 f.

a remoteness of the academic teacher education from practical issues has been countered with the measure that teacher education programs cannot be reduced to give tools and instruments for a successful professional praxis, as it is e.g. the case when teacher education is designed as a training[38] almost devoid of theoretical background.[39]

In current public and scientific debates the topic of a practical relevance of school and teacher education has become more important. This is a reaction to the development of the global labor market and an answer to the results of the international "PISA-studies". They were issued in 2000 for the first time, causing a vast reform pressure in the field of education in many nations. The question how to intensify the practical relevance of teacher education today even dominates the debates of education. Today, this question plays a central role in education theory, research and policy in Europe as well as worldwide.[40] As a consequence formal education is successively modularized and put together to "education packages". Besides, tools for the output-oriented control of school and academic teaching are developed.

There is a grand scale attempt to control academic teaching departing from its contents by means of metrical course evaluations. In this treatise it will be argued for the hypothesis that, as a result of the recent development, academic freedom and the options of Higher Education Didactics are actually reduced instead of being enlarged.[41] Furthermore, the new agencies of control promote the exclusion of university teaching from its involvement in relevant ongoing scientific research.[42]

The orientation of teacher education towards science is a phenomenon of modern times and it is, as already pointed out, controversially discussed and differently interpreted. On a large scale it has been and is understood in the sense of scientifically founded legitimation knowledge; it is also proved that teachers do not so much explain their activity-relevant, but their legitimation knowledge.[43]

---

38 Cf. tests and programs like "Fit for being a professional teacher (FIT-L)" and FIBEL-test.
39 Cf. the core curriculum of the German Association of Educational Research (DGfE) for the degree courses on Educational Sciences of the year 2001. For the structure of teacher education in Germany (bachelor and master, former bakkalaureus magister) see: The Board of the German Association of Educational Research (DGfE) ed. 2005.
40 Cf. EQR 2008: ec.europa.eu/eqf/documentation_en.htm.
41 Cf. MEYER-GUCKEL 2014, p. 34
42 Latterly, the promotion of the exclusion of the German university teaching from its involvement in ongoing scientific research is supported, e.g. by an increased adoption of employments with a high lecturing load.
43 Pointed out and criticized e.g. by KÖNIG & ZEDLER 2002, p. 2.

Only recently exercises of scientific methods have been brought up that can be used by the teachers-to-be to gain new insights and research results and also to critisize them. Increasingly, the aptitude for a scientifically reflected formation of experience is regarded as a central purpose of education in general.[44] This is not least true for a transparent and verifiable bottom-up development of teaching and school that is increasingly recognized as a need. This implies that the practical, theoretical and the scientific foundations of school education are increasingly reflected and examined in a formalized way.[45] As a recent phenomenon, the teachers shall also be enabled to "expertise"[46]. Strikingly, nowadays the significance of the professional ethics of a teacher is more apparent than other models (cf. the discussion about the "excellent teacher", the "good school", "excellent teaching").

However, either in terms of legitimation knowledge as a scientifically reflected formation of experience and expertise, or as the idea of "excellent practice", in operative regards one discusses mainly the following models and aspects of a scientific foundation of teacher education:

- The study courses successively get modularized and aligned in terms of different directions of specialization.
- The scientific orientation of teacher education is interpreted in reference to a standardized list of binding scientific literature for the academic courses.
- Teacher education is also explained as a specific Higher Education Didactics. In the framework of seminaries in teacher education at the university methods are chosen which were originally developed for education in school, or for adult education.[47] These can be environments for individual activity-oriented learning that is e.g. based on cognition-psychological or constructivistic learning theories.[48] In the diverse Subject Didactics at universities one has developed approaches to a guidance of the students in order to make the professional perspective of a specialist subject teacher accessible to them in an anticipating way and as near to reality as possible.[49] Other models for the approaches of Higher Education Didactics are oriented at (learning) biogra-

---

44 Cf. HERZOG 2005, p. 314; he refers to VON FELTEN 2005 and HERZOG & VON FELTEN 2001.
45 Cf. GIBBS 2013
46 Cf. MAYR & NEUWEG 2006
47 Cf. e.g. STELZER-ROTHE 2005
48 For environments for individual activity-oriented learning that are explained by cognition-psychological or constructivistic learning theories one can give the example of "problem-based-learning", in which cases are processed (see e.g. WEBER 2005).
49 Cf. MEYER 2003 for Art Didactics, WESTPHAL (2004) for Drama Pedagogy.

phies of the teacher students in terms of certain professional tasks. Theoretical models are often illustrated by practice examples, sometimes also by studies of individual cases. Besides that, the individual approaches of the pupils to their studies at university, to their own scientific work and to the professional practice in future are analyzed and modeled. This is done e.g. with a personality-related psychological perspective and with a view that is focused on certain topics, e.g. "gender".[50] One should not forget pedagogically founded methods, e.g. such of experiental education.[51] Such approaches focus on single aspects of the teacher personality and on the professional competences of a teacher. They underline school pedagogical or special subject-didactical topics.

- Then there are smaller, location-based reform projects that are at times evaluatively investigated. Such projects are, for example, the development of interdisciplinary courses or approaches to an improvement of the cooperation of different partner institutions of teacher education in its different phases. There are also diverse reforms of study regulations that shall e.g. contribute to an improved integration of the practical studies in school into the first period of teacher education at the university.[52]
- In different forms of a scientific follow-up of the practices of professional teachers, e.g. in projects of action research, in supervisions and/or evaluation studies one sees viable approaches to a scientifically reflected formation of experience. Some of these studies are conducted by students in the frame of teacher education programs at the university. Besides that, in recent years trainee teachers are increasingly involved into the projects of a quality development at their training schools.
- Primarily, in the frame of the empirical research on teaching and learning on a large scale approaches of a standardization[53] of teacher education are developed, oriented e.g. toward the research on school effectiveness.[54] These approaches are promoted over a wide area by diverse evaluation projects, in which processes of teaching and learning are investigated. This is done on the one hand in terms of influential factors on them; on the other hand their out-

---

50 Cf. FISCHER, FRIEBERTSHÄUSER & KLEINAU 1999
51 FISCHER 2006
52 STADELMANN 2006, p. 16 f.
53 Cf. TERHART 2002. "Standards" are measurable knowledge or competences and their relevance for professional acting.
54 For a survey of the instruments for a diagnosis of the professional competences of teachers see FREY 2006.

put is assessed.⁵⁵ Such standardization is today based on an operationalization of the professional ethics as well as on the statutory psychometric profile of the competences of an "excellent teacher". Specifically in the education policies and in the empirical research on education it is considered that the quality of teaching and learning in school is controllable and improvable by means of empirical results and normative policy requirements; governmental concepts are widely supposed to be the basis hereof.⁵⁶

The manifold approaches of teacher education should not hide the fact that a kind of learning that is oriented at science as well as at the professional praxis is confronted with a very fundamental problem: The role of theory and science in the context of the measuring of the performance and the efforts of teachers is not at all clear. Besides that, the complexity of teaching practices is still scarcely modeled, or investigated. There is currently no script or model for the translation efforts of theoretical into practical contexts and vice versa. These translation efforts are moreover in a way prescribed by the fact that a skilled acting and judging of a pro-

---

55 Klaus-Jürgen TILLMANN (2006) shows that the term of education, which is, according to the tradition of Neohumanism, an individual, reflexive process aiming at the development of an independent thinking and to an emancipatory responsibility, is inappropriately reduced in the orientation at the output of so called educational standards (in German: Bildungsstandards). – He writes: "One can raise serious doubts that the term *Bildungsstandards* [stressed by K.-J.T.] is really adequate – or whether one should not more correctly and more modestly speak of standards" (TILLMANN 2006, p. 29 f., transl. by A.K.).

56 See e.g.: www.bmbf.de/de/6880.php [latest access: 10.03.2015]. In terms of the standard-based education reforms in the first hand the "No Child Left Behind Act" (NCLB) was most influential in the world. It is a United States Act of Congress, initiated by George BUSH in 2001, which is based on the premise that setting high standards and establishing measurable goals can improve the individual outcome in education (see: www2.ed.gov/nclb/landing.jhtml [latest access: 10.03.2015]). In the NCLB Act the American government gets a power of influence of a Taylorist character on the schools (cf. WALDOW 2014). Taylorism is a form of scientific management, developed in the 19th Century by F.W. TAYLOR (1856–1915) with the main objective to improve economic efficiency, especially labor productivity by the analysis and the synthesization of workflow. Taylorism was one of the earliest attempts to apply scientific approaches to the engineering of processes and to management; it aims at a process control of work procedures, results and products in the sense of detailed specifications of working tasks and methods as "one best way", the times and places are layed down, there is an one-way-communication with fixed and narrow contents, detailed objectives leading to company goals that are not identifiable for the single acting person. Besides that, there is an external (quality) control.

fessional teacher is seen as a mere result of an academic study program. However, there is no model for this. The task of a transfer of theory to practice and vice versa is moreover "wildly" left to the practitioners, who, obviously, just have to persist and function in school after their academic studies.

The reason for this rather striking desideratum of research needs a further analysis:

- The quantitative paradigm of research is dominating the field of the sciences that focus on education. However, this paradigm does not thematize the development of didactical and process-oriented pedagogical approaches.[57]
- In general, scientific research is ruled by a strong mandate for objectivity, freedom from value judgement and validity, while teaching has a moreover subjective, normative and situated character. However, assessment in school uses quantitative test apparatūs without satisfying its scientific requirements.
- The desideratum may come from the fact that a linkage of theoretical with practical approaches to education in the frame of teacher education is often reduced to the instruction of using "[…] simple instruments for teaching"[58]. This is regarded as an inadequate and also undesirable technological or praxeological shortening of the theory-practice relation in the pedagogical field. Thus, one can read in the core curriculum[59] of the German Association of Educational Research (DGfE) for the degree courses on Educational Sciences of the year 2004: "The difference between scientific insights and professional practical knowledge should not be blurred. One should clearly mark out this difference in order to prevent technologically shortened concepts of the theory-praxis relation."[60]
- The rejection of teacher education programs of professional practice is backed up by the argument that the reflexive knowledge[61], imparted in the frame of

---

57 In the context of the noematic theory of science the reasons for this will be explicated.
58 BLÖMEKE 1998, p. 15
59 In the different German states actually special core curricula for teacher education are worked out. Until this is finished, the validity of the core curriculum of the German Association of Educational Research (DGfE) for the degree courses on Educational Sciences of the year 2004 is extended to the diverse teacher education programs.
60 DGfE 2004, p. 2, transl. by A.K.
61 This hypthesis is e.g. represented by the research on the use of knowledge in professional contexts (in German: Verwendungsforschung) within the sociologically oriented Educational Sciences that came up in the 1980ies. After certain precursory phenomena this scientific discipline is part of a paradigm shift in the self-image of Social Sciences: On one hand research subjects, or settings are seen as addressees, which

the studies at university, should moreover be bound to a discharge of professional practical decisions and any compulsion for action. It is argued that there is no, or, if yes, only an involuntary and incidental education to the "right" and "excellent" pedagogical practice in the framework of the seminars at the university. At university moreover one deals with the aspects of the future professional work field in a theoretical way; recently, on a (more or less) scientific level, empirical studies on education are carried out within the academic courses.[62] The task of an educational or didactical practice, however, is left up to the practitioners in school. The school teachers are mainly responsible for the efforts and results in school and they have to figure out the developmental perspectives connected to their teaching.[63]

- The hypothesis of a stability of professional action may serve as an argument for the idea not to develop the practical knowledge of the teaching profession through scientifically generated knowledge.[64] The quality of the work of a teacher is then seen as mainly dependent of her/his personality and her/his normative orientations and routines. Heinz-Elmar TENORTH (2006) characterizes this as "professional schemes", but not as available "knowledge". The rich experiences and the expertise of teachers are then interpreted in terms of talent and capability. There may be the option to initiate learning from a role model in the framework of a classical relationship of master and learner. However, scientific knowledge, in this case, is even considered as hindering the performance of a professional teacher.[65] In this regard one argues primarily with insurmountable differences between the explicit scientific knowledge and the practical knowledge that is needed to organize the relevant working activities.[66] Then the tasks of teacher education are, as a rule, regarded as the development of cognitive structures and as a qualitative reorganization and extension of the experience that is necessary for the discharge of the professional

---

have to be "served" with scientifically proven knowledge (science is then seen as a type of service; as e.g. contract research). On the other hand other formats of knowledge in the social world are recognized, which may follow dynamics of their own. Both of these formats of knowledge are acknowledged as important subjects of research. (Cf. BECK & BONSS 1989)

62 DEWE 1997, p. 230
63 Cf. the often cited, biggest ever evidencebased research project in education of John HATTIE, published in 2008.
64 Cf. NEUWEG 2010
65 Cf. NEUWEG 2005
66 Cf. NEUWEG 2010

functions.[67] Learning these functions and tasks is attributed to the different phases of teacher education and thereby to the diverse dedicated educational institutions. The academic-theoretical studies at the university are followed by the phase of a traineeship in terms of a successive formation of professional schemes of action; finally in the framework of the regular professional activity a skilled and flexible, implicitly operative knowledge is supposed to be attained.[68] Gathering scientific knowledge is moreover regarded as independent from such a formation of experience, although in some cases pedagogical practical experiences are seen as conductive for a career in scientific pedagogy.

- Fifth, since in many approaches efforts in transforming theories into praxis are seen as necessary for the formation of the practical and orientative knowledge of teachers,[69] often the consequence is drawn that reflexivity in the professional field of a teacher is scarcely reconstruable in its details, or even only rudimentarily available. It is more or less regularly reduced to lesson planning and reflection. In special, the observation is attested that teachers sporadically take scientific results into account in order to legitimate their own practitioning. However, it is verifiable that, normally, scientific results hardly enter the professional field of teaching. In this regard this profession differs from other professional fields (such as medicine etc.), which also have the possibility of a scientific back-up and firmly expect the impact of the scientific advance on the orientations of the professionals.[70]

In the following, reasons for the partial ignorance of professional teachers of science will be outlined:

- In practical regards the pressure of everyday decision and action that is significant for the teaching profession hinders an orientation toward scientific thinking and results. According to the "ethics of practicability" practical solutions and "simple explanations" for complex situations in school are preferred to the theories that count on analyses, reflection and critique.
- Human thinking has developed in different directions, the scientific way is only one of them.[71] Scientific disciplines define their own themes, scopes for thinking and acting as well as the processing methods. The stock of scientific

---

67 Cf. BROMME 1992
68 Cf. DREYFUS & DREYFUS 1987
69 Cf. COMBE & KOLBE 2004
70 In this regard the everyday performance of the teachers is regarded as semi-professional (cf. MEYER 2000).
71 Cf. e.g. FEYERABEND 1975

knowledge is different from other forms of knowledge, e.g. from the reflexivity regarding practices in school. Scientifically identifiable, instrumental-strategic and/or accountable-planned action and regulated procedures in the teaching profession do not play the same role as in other professions. Since cognitive rationality, control and regulation are the benchmarks of science, they do not adequately respect the special "dignity"[72] of pedagogical practices that are focused more on intuitively balancing and tempering diverse kinds of calamities. In this respect, science cannot expect a good resonance from the pedagogues, respectively from the school teachers.

- At times it is apparent that the practitioning of teachers does not need any scientific reflexivity to reach its objectives. Moreover, procedural and conditional knowledge plays the central role for the decisions of teachers, who continually and ad hoc balance out whether a certain action or decision is adequate and how it can be normatively legitimated.[73]
- Furthermore, the often contra-intuitive character of scientific insights is rather far from the intuitive practitioning of teachers.
- Even if theoretical as well as practical knowledge often appears at the same time in an educational situation, these formats of knowledge do not match in every case. It is quite common to refer this inconsistency to a presumed ignorance, inability and missing competence of the teacher. However, a gap between the theoretical knowledge and action knowledge and abilities can also be caused by complications in overcoming the difficulties of a verbalization of the "tacit"[74] aspects of a pedagogical situation. A more convincing reason for the gap are thus the unlike degrees of reflexivity of the different formats of knowledge.
- The competence of teachers to take up scientifically generated, *new* knowledge may not appear as urgent as in other professional fields, because the professional performance does not entail (visible) bad risks, crises or extraordinary disturbances with possibly disastrous results, as it is the case in other professional fields.

---

72 "The dignity of practice is independent of theory; practice only becomes more conscious with theory" (SCHLEIERMACHER 1957, p. 11, transl. by A.K.).
73 Cf. WULF & ZIRFAS 2007, p. 12. The procedural knowledge (to know *how*) includes the implicit knowledge about procedures and actions that follow strict rules as well as knowledge of action in general; the conditional knowledge (know, *when*) refers to the conditions of the application of knowledge as well as to the situational relevance of certain abilities. (Cf. BLOOM 1973 and see above)
74 See: http://tacitdimensionsjournal.wordpress.com/ [latest access: 10.03.2015]

- The teaching practice is determined by manifold normative provisions, in special, such of education policy, or economics of education that are arranged to the practitioners in school as their frames of orientation. Scientific approaches are thus only one of the potentially normatively effective instances in this professional field.

In any case teachers will very likely continue to use mainly everyday concepts to reflect on their teaching, as long as the transformation of theory to praxis in this field and vice versa is not scientifically modeled, investigated and imparted in the frame of teacher education.

Furthermore, it becomes apparent that a processing of this desideratum of teacher education oriented at the pedagogical praxis as well as at scientific research might not at last include a new understanding of fundamental education-theoretical and -scientific approaches.[75]

The topic of this essay is the fundamental question: what is the relation between science and the practices in school, including the reflexivity of these practices. It will be answered, at first, in a rather simple way.

Relatively often one comes across the opinion that scientific theories and results in this professional field are deemed as inadequate to their objectives. This opinion is explained and testified in many different ways.

Dona M. KAGAN (1992) proved empirically that the basic views and forms of action of teachers are based on typified patterns of perception, interpretation and action, which only subsequently are linked to their own theories. In the view of this finding she puts the relevance of a theoretical formation of teachers fundamentally in question.[76] Ewald TERHART et al. (1994) presented the empirical result stating that the teachers practice their own professional reality even without any conscious, verbalized and available knowledge of their patterns of action. Karin NÖLLE (2004) shows that only 7% of the well-trained teacher staff she interviewed refer to evidence-based knowledge. This leads her even to the conclusion that lay people are examined in the framework of teacher education.

However, these authors assume that the practices in the teaching profession contain theory, but they consider this to be of minor importance. The low social

---

75 One can easily find more counter-examples. E.g. the "work process analysis" (WPA) that calculates "typical professional tasks" (TPTs) and connects this to research on different professional profiles (cf. MEYER 2000). However, these approaches do as a rule not take science-theoretical considerations into account. In the frame of research on the use of knowledge in professional contexts mainly the question of the possibilities and means of a scientific investigation are focused.

76 KAGAN 1992, p. 163

prestige of teacher education corresponds with their estimation.[77] Seen from their perspective, there is thus hardly an option of a scientific and theory-based propedeutics of the professional practices of teachers in the classroom.

Sharon FEIMAN-NEMSER & Margret BUCHMANN (1986) argue quite differently. They moreover view the foundation of teacher education in terms of helping "[…] prospective teachers make a complex conceptual shift from common-sense to professional views of teaching."[78] They see the purpose of (teacher) education, respectively of a scientifically reflected formation of experience in the systematic questioning and restructuring of everyday knowledge.[79] They differentiate this task in the reflection of learning conditions and processes on one hand, and on the other hand in the reflection of the subjects on teaching and on didactical-methodical settings.

The two very disparate concepts are both extremes of a whole range of other interpretations of the theory-practice relation in question. The idea of a hardly surmountable gap between the practical and the theoretical knowledge[80] is in any case not an inevitable fact, but the gap is based in discursively generated, argumentatively structured considerations.[81] However, there is already a certain overturning of the presumption of this gap.

Bernd DEWE (1997) e.g. shows in regard of school reports and lesson plans made in the framework of the practical training in school that the teacher students very well applied scientific theories to the observations and experiences they made during their traineeship in order to justify their practicioning. He describes the link between theory and practice as a central challenge to the professional

---

[77] Cf. the historical lines that are presented above. Besides that, the so called "teacher deficit viewpoint" and the "accountability perspective" is of importance in this context. These views are criticized by Richard INGERSOLL (2003, p. 100) in the following way: The habitus behind it "[…] offers only a partial, one-sided explanation, and, as a result, the reforms often do not work, but can even make things worse." He refuses the public and "sociological imagination" instead, and marks out the problems of the teachers as a general social challenge.

[78] FEIMAN-NEMSER & BUCHMANN 1986, p. 240

[79] Cf. HERZOG & VON FELTEN 2001

[80] Cf. the hypothesis of a "practice shock", brought up by Gisela MÜLLER-FOHRBRODT et al. (1978), is seen by some authors as excessive and inappropriate. Obviously a *phase of the overburdening* the new teacher experiences when entering the profession is not suffered by all newcomers and, if this is the case, it is experienced differently in its intensity. However, the desideratum is not closed by this restriction.

[81] The terms of discourse and discourse analysis will be explained below.

practice, e.g. in the framework of academic courses on teaching practice.[82] Robert FAUX (2000) proves for the discipline of Educational Psychology that the students were able to apply their theoretical knowledge to the professional practice, respectively to special case studies.[83]

There are certainly many other examples of a scientific evidence of such "wild", because not precisely theoretically and scientifically designated efforts of transforming theory to practice and vice versa. As their process structure is more or less hidden, these efforts are also only more or less successful in practice.

We already mentioned above that, if these transformation efforts will be continually insufficiently scientifically reflected, modeled and thematised in the frame of teacher education at the university, the problematic assumption will be continued that the teacher trainees on their own possess the intellectual capabilities and the operative schemes that are necessary in professional regards. This assumption can be applied for the traineeship as well as for the learner-oriented, didactical, pedagogical and situation-specific professional work as a teacher. In some cases there is the additional assumption that the students acquire these abilities automatically in the context of their practical activities.

Generalizable practical schemes of teaching are indeed not proven.[84] Therefore, it is unlikely that the ability of the students to apply scientific-theoretical findings to the professional field can be systematically trained in terms of improving the professional practice. A special challenge in the teaching profession is the fact that the teacher is considerably affected by his/her own professional acting and decisions. That is to say, the teacher does not only *plan* her/his teaching, but s/he also *reacts* on the diverse effects of her/his own utterings and actions and on social happenings in general. Most of the interactions taking place in a classroom can hardly be reflected beforehand, they are moreover incidents or episodes, or they are learning results. Thus, the studies e.g. by KAGAN (1992), TERHART et al. (1994) and NÖLLE (2004) mark out categorical knowledge only as a small part of the orientative and the practical knowledge of teachers. Therefore, our argumentation should go along with these studies, but definitely not be ruled out by their arguments.

In the following, we deal with the forms and formats of knowledge that may be expected to play a decisive role for the teaching profession. In this context also the question arises, how these forms and formats of knowledge can be anticipated scientifically and how they can be reflected and trained.

---

82 Cf. DEWE 1997, p. 227
83 FAUX 2000
84 This is not the case e.g. according to the study of TERHART et al. (1994).

"Format of knowledge" means the principal dependence of certain knowledge on the way *how* it is known. Knowledge is thus *available* as knowledge formats. It is submitted to contextualizations that are as well negotiated as mediated by and in a knowledge format. An example of this is the knowledge about the social implications of domestic waste and the ecological knowledge about it: what is seen as socially intolerable from one perspective (waste in public spaces) is, from another perspective, seen as a valuable recycling material. – Knowledge formats are indicated differently: for example the first mentioned format of knowledge can be shown in a distorted grimace, and a recycling code illustrates the other one. In terms of knowledge formats not only explicit, but also implicit ones play an important role. Whereas the recycling code is a legal convention, the social implications of domestic waste are a result of mostly implicit processes of socialization. The significations of waste thus change from one context to the other.

At times, in pedagogical fields the different forms and formats of knowledge conflict with each other (such as the knowledge about integration and that about selection in school), and they cause tensions. It appears that in the everyday professional practices of decision-making and action especially implicit forms of knowledge play a central role.

This perspective follows and goes along with the development of postmodern and poststructuralist theories in the course of the so called "linguistic turn", which describes the relation of human-beings to themselves and to the world by means of language. Here, a persistent opposition to universals has been established. Especially the "grand narratives", such as the fundamental principles brought up by the Enlightenment have been undermined. Jean-Francois LYOTARD ([1979] 1984) points at the modern alertness to difference and diversity instead, and stresses the incompatibility of our aspirations, beliefs and desires. He characterises postmodern thinking by the abundance of micro-narratives and by different forms of knowledge. Different forms of knowledge are to be recognised in their own right, in terms of language games and as forms of the discourse that are in conflict with each other.[85]

We start from the hypothesis that the endeavor to forward the practical professionalization in teaching by a practically as well as scientifically reflected formation of experience is in the first hand determined by the parallels and the differences of the practical and orientative knowledge of the teachers and the knowledge of the scientists. That is to say, we focus on a propedeutics of the knowledge formats that are important for a professionalization in teaching. Supposingly, this knowledge is not so much oriented at scientific knowledge as such, but needs a special science.

---

85 Cf. MEDER 1996

To develop scholarly principles in teacher education it is of importance to at first work on the parallels and the differences between practical and scientific knowledge formats.

1.3 The Relation of Theory and Practice in Professional Teaching and its Relation to Scientific Approaches

There is, as e.g. Walter HERZOG (2007) points out, no fundamental difference(s) between "theory" and "practice" in general. The separation of "theory" and "practice" moreover has historical, cultural, discursive and conceptual reasons and is in general founded in the history of ideas.

Teacher education is not seldom, e.g. by Paul TROWLER & Roni BAMBER (2005), accused of ignorance of the disciplinary borders and of a missing consensus about the definition of the relation between reflexive practice and scientific research.[86] Therefore, Georg H. NEUWEG (2010, at first 2005) sums up a broad range of different concepts of the theory-practice relation in teacher education. He, in a systematic way, distinguishes so called "difference" from "integration" concepts: While "integration" concepts assume a congruence of practitioning and knowledge in the field of the teaching profession, the "difference" concepts underline the distinct internal logics of the two professional areas and assign pedagogical theories a low relevance for educational practices. NEUWEG (2010) situates twelve possible standpoints on the imaginary line between the maximum of "integration" (respectively congruency of theory and practice in the teaching profession) and a maximum of a "difference" between both. In terms of the question of this essay only three (the options 3, 4 and 5) of the following six concepts of "integration" will be in focus:

1) The most "integrative" option argues by thinking that teachers in general are capable of doing what they theoretically know; accordingly, the professional mentors in the field comment and grasp theoretically what they perform competently.
2) Another approach follows the hypothesis that a systematic analysis of scientific theories should start from the so called "subjective theories"[87] of the teachers

---

86 TROWLER & BAMBER 2005 p. 84
87 Cf. GROEBEN & SCHEELE 1982; SCHEIRING 1998. "Subjective theories", also those of scientific researchers, are generally considered as an important topic of research, especially in the field of qualitative Social Research (e.g. according to the Grounded Theory).

about teaching and learning in school, regarded as their professional knowledge. In order to exercise professional knowledge in the framework of teacher education the "subjective theories" of the practitioners (students or professional teachers) are theoretically reflected.

3) "Inert knowledge" is supposed to be prevented by a systematic attainment of knowledge and by a targeted training of perception and comportment;
4) The bridging of the gap between abstract knowledge and acting in concrete situations is conceptionalized e.g. as "pedagogical tactus"[88], "pedagogical judgment" and "application competence". The central challenge to teachers is to make different perceptions and judgments compatible. In the framework of teacher education this mostly implicit pedagogical knowledge is considered as best learned by means of case studies;
5) According to perception-theoretical approaches a professionalization of teachers can be reached by recurring to theoretical knowledge in working on the patterns of meaning and thinking underlying professional practitioning;[89]
6) The "technology model"[90] displays general, empirically proven operational rules in distance to situative contexts and to everyday knowledge. In successful teaching these rules are supposed to be followed up. Operational rules are learnt in the framework of a theoretical phase of academic studies previously to the professional training.

In this essay the view of different "integration" concepts is shared that the translation, or transformation of educational as well as of cultural theories into the professional practice is not only possible, but simply conventional. Here it will be argued within a triangle of three of NEUWEG's (2010) models for teacher education: We will operate with the view of "inert knowledge" as well as with concepts about bridging the gap between abstract knowledge and concrete situations. Furthermore, we see working on the patterns of meaning and thinking underlying professional practitioning as an adequate route to bridging the gap between educational theory and practice.

---

[88] NEUWEG (2010) refers the term "pedagogical tact" to NOHL 1997.
[89] Cf. VAN MANEN 1995
[90] In the scientific literature the technology concept of Didactics and teacher education in general is profiled with respect to both of the rationales, the "integration" and the "difference" concepts.

1.3.1 Practical Knowledge and the Orientation of Teachers in Comparison with Scientific Approaches

Both work fields, the scientific approaches to education in school and the educational practice in school, here interpreted in terms of its propedeutics (teacher education), tend to a certain self-reference, and they get their stability and reliability primarily by self-legitimation.

In the case of the practices in school and a ("life-long") teacher education, this form of legitimation can be interpreted as an aspect of the "dignity of practice"; whereas the sciences are considered as critical per se.[91] In the case of scientific reflexivity the critique of its self-reference is reflected within the diverse theories of knowledge developed within the Science Studies. A critique of school practice is referred to its scientific foundations.

The reflexivity in both of the professional fields is thus directed towards science. Scientific results are supposed to be part of a subsequent teacher education.

In principal, science and school practice, also teacher education, follow different rules. They do not require the same competences and they differ in their implicit relations as well as in their explicit references to their respective contexts. The practices in both fields are not only backed by different knowledge formats, they also have different aims and effects. Besides that, there are different instances of reglementation and critique. In the following, the two professional fields will be defined according to the patterns of practice and general framings typical for them.

School knowledge is defined by laws, state curricula, school books etc. mainly in terms of coherent and complete subject areas and specialist competences. In classes individual access to learning and the reflection of it is to be made possible, mostly by recurring to well-prepared knowledge formats. The reflexive and orientative knowledge of teachers is thus, as a rule, in the first hand directed to their lesson planning and to their school practice with all its rationales and legitimations. An informed, thoughtful and rational lesson planning is desiable, in which well-targeted, scientifically reasonable goals are linked to didactical considerations.

However, the significance and meaning of teaching and learning in school is not given by these plannings. Sense, however, derives primarily from the active participation in, and the contribution of the acting persons to a lesson. Sense arises when the pupils and the teacher join into common learning-teaching-experienc-

---

91 Cf. DERRIDA [1998] 2002

es. The significance and meaning of school teaching is thus generated in manifold ways and situationally by the various agents and under specific circumstances.

Scientific research is principally free in the way of having its purpose in itself.[92] In science the focus is on the field and on the objects of research. Scientific fields and objects decide on scientific methods and processes, and vice versa. Such a decision is done on a theoretical and methodological level.

The legitimation of the Educational Sciences is thus certainly not a matter of practical pedagogy. In our case the reality of school and lessons in school or school policies cannot serve as a legitimation for scientific theories and results. A (critical) basic research as well as a wide range of scientific topics and approaches is (at least today and in liberal countries) legitimate and/or customary.

While scientific studies on education in school often focus on the lesson planning, it is generally accepted that the reflexivity behind the success of professional teaching is not least rational and planned, but rather well-informed and mostly

---

92 In terms of contractual, directly application-oriented research, values and norms of research as well as the political control of science are, however, on the daily agenda. An example is the "framework-programme of the German Federal Ministry of Education and Research for Support of Empirical Research on Education (BMBF)" (in German: "Rahmenprogramm des BMBF zur Förderung the empirischen Bildungsforschung", transl. by A.K.). Here one can read: "Systems of education and of science increasingly become central factors in the international competition. The new public government of the education system, which is data-based and result-oriented, needs an effective empirical research on education. The framework-programme of the BMBF shall help to structurally strengthen the empirical research on education in Germany, to develop it qualitatively and to crosslink it more strongly internationally, to provide knowledge for a reform of the systems of education and science, and to sound central instruments of output and evidence-based politics (educational standards; comparative assessment; external evaluation of schools; educational reporting) scientifically." In German: "Bildungs- und Wissenschaftssysteme werden zunehmend zu zentralen Faktoren im internationalen Wettbewerb. Die neue Steuerung im Bildungssystem, die datenbasiert und ergebnisorientiert ist, braucht eine leistungsfähige empirische Bildungsforschung. Das Rahmenprogramm des BMBF soll dazu beitragen, empirische Bildungsforschung in Deutschland strukturell zu stärken, qualitativ zu entwickeln und stärker international zu vernetzen, Wissen für die Reform des Bildungs- und Wissenschaftssystems bereitzustellen, zentrale Instrumente einer output- und evidenzbasierten Politik (Bildungsstandards; Leistungsvergleiche; externe Evaluation von Schulen; Bildungsberichterstattung) wissenschaftlich zu fundieren." Source: http://www.empirische-bildungsforschung-bmbf.de/ [access on 08.07.2012]; later only: www.schulweb.de/de/seiten/drucken.html?seite=6106 [latest access: 10.03.2015]

intuitive, situative and functional.[93] Significant for teaching in school is foremost the so called "pedagogy on the threshold"[94], respectively the designing of a lesson in school at the very moment of entering the classroom. Significantly there is no scientific term for the situational and reflexively not easily graspable "pedagogy on the threshold", discrediting in a way the focus of scientific research on lesson planning. However, it is up to the teachers to continuously create a pedagogical situation in the framework of the school, respectively to realize and professionally influence the special learning conditions of the pupils in terms of reaching the objectives that are distinctly set for their learning and for the teaching. The central task of teachers is to constantly provide for and to structure opportunities to learn in a formal way. This involves the choice of specialized subject contents, of processes and procedures, a reference to regulative-social and philosophical ideas as well as a focus on such objectives and values that are directly related to the individuals (e.g. to the ability of someone to make a decision on a specialist topic). Commonly, the teacher teaches and the pupils are supposed to actively undergo learning processes. Then, it is central to classes that the teacher makes the contents compatible with the diverse previous experiences of the individuals as well as with their actual learning situation. In order to meet these requirements, the professional has to ascertain the structures of the many parallel and overlapping activities in a group of learners. The teacher coordinates these activities and restructures and promotes them towards the common aim. Each pupil should be able to reach this aim. Therefore, the teacher focusses the significance and the meanings the pupils and s/he share in terms of the topic of the lesson; creating meaning thus forms the steady center of a class. Accompanying her/his teaching and her/his educative practices by reflexion, the teacher analyses the complex events in the classroom and in school according to developmental categories of learning, personality and behavior. S/he continually coordinates the results of this analysis with her/his ongoing didactical analysis of the subject, or topic and with her/his (e.g. pedagogical) coordination work related to this as well as with the logistics necessary for it. The teacher reconciles the results of her/his didactics and diagnostics also with the constitution of a sense that surmounts the actual situation in order to be able to check, whether her/his general social and interpersonal, pedagogical, disciplinary and didactical objectives are met. If this is not the case, s/he finds alternative paths of initiating learning. The challenge of initiating learning, of approving and of assessing the learning processes requires a perception that is thus directed to the very objectives of a lesson as well as to general educational objectives. Besides that,

---

93   E.g. Neuweg 2005
94   In German: Schwellenpädagogik

the ability is needed to reflect the statements of the different acting persons and to align them with common objectives and, as far as possible, also with a collectively shared meaning. Such a meaning is, in the best case, the very topic or subject of a class, underpinned by general and special educational objectives. However, there is no other way for the teacher than to derive her/his didactical and pedagogical considerations from her/his anticipations of such a creation of a common meaning.[95] However, these anticipations can only be of a rough and limited character. However, the teacher analyses the communicative processes in the classes, while being involved in them and even controlling them. S/he analyses these processes with the aim to set the accents necessary for making desired learning processes most likely to occur. This implies the ability to reflect actually applied or upcoming knowledge formats in terms of their relevance to the special topic of the lesson. Manifold knowledge formats (not only cognitive-rational ones) must be at the disposal for the teacher, and s/he must be able to interpret them in terms of their potentials for learning and of the actual educational situation. The teacher must thus be able to apply the formats of knowledge mutatis mutandis. The synchronous arising of the different forms and formats of knowledge can be mastered only situationally. Besides that, various transformations of one form or format of knowledge into another have to be done.

To perceive, reflect, exercise and deepen these processes of creating meaning is a central task for the lifelong learning of a teacher. In science, forms and formats of knowledge are topics of research; they are scarcely seen as the subject matters of the development of competences and of a lifelong learning of the scientists.[96] Scientific knowledge is moreover understood as rational; and rational comprehensibility is a binding benchmark for the quality of scientific work. Scientific knowledge bases are investigated systematically in terms of their gaps respectively desiderata. Scientific approaches are characterized by being proven in terms of their terminology, discursively as well as empirically, in any case methodically. Scientific knowledge tends to be highly specialized and at the same time it is partial. It is, in contrast to the professional knowledge of teachers, proven in its construction. Dependent on their theoretical, methodical and methodological frame of reference scientific approaches claim generalizability. Science primarily deals with the legitimation of its approaches, theories, views or results (e.g. such concerning the pedagogical practices). Even the theories of science are genuinely concerned about the preconditions, methods and aims of acquiring scientific knowledge,

---

95   Cf. publications on the directives of lesson planning (e.g. ESSLINGER-HINZ et al. 2007)
96   This is different in other countries, e.g. in Sweden (see e.g. ENGLUND et al. 2012, here e.g. CARLGREN 2012).

the legitimation of science is today, as a rule, not primarily science-theoretical. Moreover, it is supposed to be (merely) given by proven scientific (methodical) procedures and by their stringent methodological framing. Latterly, the rules for an external reviewing and funding of scientific research play a more and more important role in science.

Teachers, in turn, cannot all alone define and interpret their field of work and influence. They are, moreover, always a part of a more or less unspecific sociality and they are under a polymorphous pressure to justify their practices in ethical, moral, disciplinary and pedagogical regards, at times also materially. This pressure to justify everything has its origins in the fact that the didactical and pedagogical responsibility of teachers is per se linked to ethical values, Dieter-Jürgen LÖWISCH (2000) interprets teaching competences in general as "[...] accurate, appreciable[97] practices and as a practitioning that is bound to a personal responsible attitude"[98]. Pedagogical and didactical acting is directed to reaching the highest possible degree of appropriateness in terms of the learners, the subject matter in question and the normative factors effecting school practice.[99] There is the necessity, or even the pressure to justify the professional action as well ex ante as in duratio and ex post; this justification is processed implicitly as well as explicitly. In the professional field of teachers, distinct and diffuse, durable and temporary, political as well as interpersonal fights about decisions, power and resources show effects.

The (partially for the teacher imponderable) normative framings of pedagogy in school can be differentiated as follows:

- First, the interpretation of a situation by a teacher is determined by her/his own, often unreflected experiences, ideas, dispositions, and her/his ethical and moral principles as well as by her/his spontaneous values and by benchmarks s/he sets by acting and deciding.
- Second, the situational dispositions of the pupils, their practices, ideas and attitudes and their perspectives of development are normative directions for school practices. To take them into account is in the center of the professional practitioning of teachers.

---

97   The appreciation of acting in this professional field is decided by the criterium of the action relevance of information. Cf. the definition of information as "knowledge in action" by the information scientist KUHLEN (1991).
98   LÖWISCH 2000, p. 129, transl. by A.K.
99   The rules valid for school in general, for the segregated school system in special, for the work market, for the expectations of parents, or for the spatial conditions of school lessons are such external factors governing teaching and learning in school.

- Third, colleagues, parents, school management, or school supervision are authorized in various ways to approve education and teaching. However, the concepts of education, learning and socialization of these different groups may substantially stand in conflict with each other. Such conflicts are often stated directly in social situations; sometimes they are dismissed, repressed, or they arise as sublime social, or even inner conflicts, like e.g. moral dilemmata or conflicts of loyalty.
- Fourth, formal working conditions are normative framings for school and classes. One may think e.g. of employment contracts, resolutions, provisions and public calls, the organization and culture of a school, formal interventionist actions, supralocal measurements and their effects.
- Fifth, binding curricula, textbooks, governmental documents, etc. define what counts as school knowledge in terms of consistent, coherent and structured concepts, fixed knowledge stocks and formats, recommending not least the facilitation of individual approaches to learning.
- Sixth, manifold societal, discursively produced, e.g. social orientative models that are mediated mainly by mass media play a certain role for the professional acting of teachers. Society and cultures determine interpretative patterns of behavior. In an inclusive migration society objectives are broadly diversified. They often contradict each other. However, in the classroom they have to be dealt with in an allover beneficial way.
- Seventh, scientific results and approaches are orientative and argumentative patterns for the school and the teachers. Furthermore, the analyses of the topic of a lesson (subject analysis), of the learning steps and of exercises, and the didactical considerations that are derived from these analyses have to be scientifically correct. Further scientific perspectives that are relevant for school practice are the topic of this essay.
- Eighth, the practical and orientative knowledge of teachers in their daily teaching is continuously challenged by the democratic principles and organs (also school legislation) and it is orientated at the Fundamental Rights. The interpretations of the Fundamental Rights are not merely given, but demand interpretation in a society that is characterized by pluralistic values, norms and cultures. Such an interpretation is incessantly required of a teacher and it has to be provided by her/him independently and in a practice-oriented way.

The special dignity of pedagogical practice thus consists in situation-specific copings with diverse actions and acting persons, who take part in a manifold, mutable and miscellaneous normativity, characterized by controversies and uncertainties. Accordingly, pedagogical acting is very complex. The processes of reconciliation and cooperation with different normative instances are often conducted simultaneously and they can only be reconstructed in parts. This is particularly the case since pedagogical acting is not always explicitly oriented at the diverse instances that are normatively decisive. A teacher acts as a professional when s/he recognizes as many normative framings of her/his acting as possible and serves them best in a self- and socially responsibly prioritizing way.

Science, moreover, found its ethical rules and norms on its own authority. The overall impact of science is tested by the scientific community in a discursive way and by means of diverse forms of assessment (peer review, academic qualifications, academic performance etc.).

Teachers are principally under the pressure of action and time[100], which makes it impossible always to notice all norms about their classes, much less to do them justice. Often the pressure of action and time in class is immediate, and typically produced by the pupils. In a situation of pressure of action a teacher often has to set her/his priorities differently than before, or than s/he has planned it. Thus, the criteria and maxims for action can ad hoc be put at stake and be designed and scheduled differently than before. The different teachers react in many ways to this kind of challenge. Acting under the pressure of time is often connected to delayed statements. Actions and decisions under pressure in a school practice cannot be fully reflected; sometimes they are not even explicit, or at all conscious. Often different lines of action, plots and decisions overlap each other. This may happen in a very complex way, and sometimes rapidly, subsequently and promptly. Under some circumstances the teacher is also confronted with diverse calamities. S/he has to make compromises, or to regulate the priorities in a new way. Practitioning might at times be legitimated only in a shortened, sometimes in a purely pragmatical form. Due to the time-constraints also (temporary or permanent) power interests, or social asymmetries are accepted that might not be adequate, relevant or pertinent. Some phenomena (that might be significant in educational regards) may be ignored. Regarding the interpretation of developmental tasks, ambivalent, or other inconsistent assignment logics may come into play.[101] Sometimes exclusions and reductions are carried out, or they just occur. There are situations in which the teacher cannot make a required reconciliation of interests happen in the desired manner. Also a (partial) ignorance may come up. Partially blindly and habitually controlled and only in parts consciously, the teacher continuously

---

100 Cf. WAHL 1991. Also NEUWEG (2005, 2010) points out the aspect of time pressure in his publications about the teacher profession.
101 LAMPRECHT 2012, p. 120

sets priorities, s/he develops "strategies for acting" and "survival tactics".[102] Such calculations can be of a temporary, or of a permanent character.

However, in the field of scientific work one meets the pressure of action and time polymorphously and as dependent on manifold circumstances. Scientific work takes, as a rule, a rather long time.

It should have become clear that the educational and didactical practice in school cannot, in theoretical regards, be defined in any other way than by diverse, rationally not easily resolvable fields of tension.[103]

The understanding of its own subject matter in terms of fields of tension has a long history and tradition in pedagogy.[104] It is especially striking that pedagogy is on one hand oriented at the *here and now* of the pupil; on the other hand, under a developmental perspective the options of the pupil in the future, her/his individual potentials and abilities, interests, characteristics and dispositions are estimated and assessed within pedagogy. Furthermore, the living skills as well as the utility of subjects in school and the aim of an individual development of learning can come into contradiction. In logical regards incongruent, but in practice synchronous are e.g. the assessment (only) of the required performance and the allowing of mistakes. Furthermore, the pedagogue has to balance out proximity and distance, releasing and concern, heteronomy and self-determination or participation, social commitment and freedom, critique and forbearance, over-protection and laisser-faire. All these are contradictions that inevitably arise in a pedagogical relationship and that have to be carried out in terms of initiating processes of meaning-making. The form of sense-making is constantly changing. Another field of tension is that of a semantic-symbolic and that of a practical coping with situational challenges.

Krassimir STOJANOV (2004) consequently gives the Educational Sciences (and herewith also the science-based reflexivity of the school practice) the task to differentiate the terms of antinomy[105], paradox and dilemma more clearly in a semantic way than it is now the case in specialized texts on pedagogy; he writes:

---

102 Cf. WULF & ZIRFAS 2007
103 Cf. GRUNTZ-STOLL 1999; ESSLINGER-HINZ et al. 2008. Rainer WINKEL (1988, p. 17, transl. by A.K.) writes: "One should experience limits, attachments, borders as self-determination, freedom and autonomy. Only a teacher who is able to stand ambiguities will accept this fact. – The impatient, breathless purists detest this antinomy."
104 Some of the representatives of the long pedagogical tradition of a thinking in antinomies are Rainer WINKEL (1988), in history Johann A. COMENIUS (see above), Friedrich SCHLEIERMACHER (1768–1834) and Theodor LITT (1880–1962).
105 "Antinomy", Ancient Greek ἀντί: against, νόμος: rule; in the sense "incommensurateness of rules".

"Connected to this conceptual deficit is [...] the lack of a normative differentiation of the different types of paradoxes, respectively contradictions: on one hand of such contradictions that have to be regarded as blockades for pedagogical acting and also for educational processes in general and that may have to be rendered ineffective, and on the other hand such that possibly entail dialectical potentials for development and therefore [...] should be *withstood* [accentuation by K.S.]."[106]

Some of the pedagogical fields of tension can be reduced to interpersonal differences: the pupils are different in terms of their gender, the specifics of their socialization, in terms of their socio-economical and ethnical backgrounds (in some cases these differences are hardly perceivable, in other cases very obvious). Besides that, there are differences in terms of the competence profiles and the (moral-ethical, corporal, mental etc.) level of development of the pupils. Other dissimilarities exist in terms of their states of motivation and their interests as well as regarding their possibilities and willingness to actively involve in a school lesson and in the school life – just to mention some of the interpersonal differences in the pedagogical field.

The pupils are of course different from the teacher also. The most striking difference is the difference of age. Allowing for a philosophical view on *the child* we can point out with Maurice MERLEAU-PONTY ([1945] 2005) that the child should always in a way maintain its own right in its relationship to adults; he writes: "[...] In reality, it must be the case that the child's outlook is in some way vindicated against the adult's [...], and that the unsophisticated thinking of our earliest years remains as an indispensable acquisition underlying that of maturity, if there is to be for the adult one single intersubjective world."[107]

Especially didactical arrangements for a differentiated provision[108] should meet different norms as well as contradictions and the different learning affordances of the pupils under time pressure. Such arrangements practised within

---

106 STOJANOV 2004, p. 80, transl. by A.K.
107 MERLEAU-PONTY [1945] 2005, p. 414. MERLEAU-PONTY continues: "My awareness of constructing an objective truth would never provide me with anything more than an objective truth for me, and my greatest attempt at impartiality would never enable me to prevail over my subjectivity (as Descartes so well expresses it by the hypothesis of the malignant demon), if I had not, underlying my judgements, the primordial certainty of being in contact with being itself, if, before any voluntary *adoption of a position* I were not already *situated* in an intersubjective world, and if sciences, too, were not upheld by this basic δoξα."
108 In contrast to the "external differentiation" the arrangements for a differentiated provision intend didactical settings that provide for an individual help for each single learner in a learning group. The diversity of the learning conditions, talents and interests in

the mainstream class by forming separate study groups considering the differing capabilities, are seen as the most opportune way of dealing productively with the heterogeneous learning conditions of every pupil.

The teachers represent teaching professionalism in many different ways. One teacher in some degree shares the distinguishing features of his/her pupils, whereas not in the same way as another teacher. The teachers also differ in terms of their abilities to recognize, comprehend and deal with the effects of such differences and in the way how they react on them in pedagogical, diagnostical and didactical regards. Besides that, they are different in the ways they are taking such differences into account, e.g. when assessing the students.

The demand of taking interpersonal differences into account is systematically followed up by the Children's Studies and by Pupil Research, which scientifically investigate the perspectives of the acting juveniles, and are interested in the way how they perceive a situation and how they consider it in their judgments and actions.

The investigation takes place e.g. in the sense of a "culture of (verbal) feedback", which is recently in an increasing way also cultivated in the frame of classes in school, at times as part of a didactical setting. In these contexts it is recognized e.g. that the kids cannot verbalize their own experiences of learning in an adequate way – seen from the perspective of an adult person. In order to be able to explore their perspectives, therefore, other methods are needed than those that are directed only to the adult way of a verbalization of experiences and categorical knowledge. Not least a setting of learning can serve as a method for collecting data for the Children's Studies and Pupil Research.[109]

However, the actual constructions and learning paths of the pupils in school are very often different from those the teacher assumes. Beside the official classroom practices a lot of plot sidelines come into play. Georg BREIDENSTEIN (2006) notices that children and teenagers participate in a school lesson in their role as peers as well as in their role as pupils. They thus give a profile to the class and to school in both regards. BREIDENSTEIN (2006) calls this the "pupils' job". The "pupils' job" is an instrumental and strategical relation to school, which is for the most part accepted as passable by the pupils as well as by the teachers. This role model for the pupils implies unequivocal signals of boredom and also attitudes that are definitely not connected to the official events at school. The "pupils' job" makes it possible for the pupils to *function* as pupils and at the same time to *allevi-*

---

a group of learners is seen as a desirable chance to create work cultures and a reciprocal exchange, which promote learning (cf. HINZ 1995).

[109] Cf. HEINZEL 2000

ate the tension deriving from the competitive situation which necessarily persists between the peers in terms of efforts and school success. However, the teachers count on the behavioral patterns of the "pupils' job", even if they are often confronted with this behavior in a provocative way. The "pupils' job" is in any case not identical with the generally desired, or politically designed role of a pupil.

The "pupils' job" is not least an example and a sign of the fact that school is, as a rule, determined by processes of homogenization (e.g. only a special performance counts) and thus by a certain (at times functional) blindness for the pedagogical antinomies.

In the following, the polymorphous normativity of pedagogy in school will be considered more concretely and detailled. As we already pointed out, the teachers deal with this normativity under time pressure. Thus, they have to balance over and over again between general claims and the concrete claim for individualization.

Principally, the idea of school follows that of an external homogenization of education (age cohorts, school classes, the Human Right of education etc.). The idea is that by means of orders, regulations, target groups and work units etc. pedagogical acting and decision-making, individual acting as well as collective processes and general procedures become predictable, understandable and manageable.

Thus, the creation of a pedagogical relationship to every single pupil occurs under the signs of a general probability that is generated due to specific requirements and led by general liabilities and generally accessible knowledge:

On one hand an appropriate regulatory framework makes it possible to follow up the educational purposes in terms of each single pupil, concerning also her/his claim for a specific learning support. Such requirements are e.g. the organization of the subjects in school, the constellation of the kids in a class (age-homogenous or -mixed, inclusive or segregative learning groups etc.), spatial conditions and given time structures, or similar factors and conditions.

On the other hand the singularity of a pedagogical and didactical situation, also the individuality of the participants and the general societal requirements and expectations come into contradiction with one another in many ways in educational practices.[110] The right of each pupil of integrity, individuality and per-

---

110 The singularity of an educational and didactical situation comes e.g. into conflict with the general social requirements, when individuals or social groups resist certain formalized activities in school and school lessons. However, such a protest can at times be an integral and important moment of an educational process ("Bildung"). In another case, general social requirements come into conflict with the singularity of an

sonal development are e.g. often contrary to the societal functions of the school. The school has the function to qualify the pupils in a verifiable way for certain individual undertakings and also generally for fulfilling given tasks in society (qualification). School has an allocation function, opening or closing up higher forms of education, supporting or preventing the personal persuits of the pupils as well as their professional careers.[111] School has to select the pupils in terms of their intellectual abilities and capabilities (selection). In this regard a central characteristic of school is the fact that each uttering or expression as well as the absence of expression is potentially assessed. Whether certain learning goals are reached is usually judged metrically, for each individual as well as in a generalizing way. Individual efforts in school are in most cases referred to the expectations of a learning group and they are assessed in relation to a general measurement. The depth and the extent of learning and education cannot, however, be measured and controlled by considering only the metrical output.

The agents of education and didactics are often individuals, and education is bound to singular processes and factual circumstances. Regarding the pedagogical idea of respecting differences and otherness (e.g. childlikeness) of a concrete other person is, according to Jörg Zirfas (2010), even to consider in a principal way: "Only if one starts from a radical undecidability, one can appropriately take over the responsibility for the other person."[112] According to the well-known and controversially discussed hypothesis of Philippe Ariès' (1998), the idea of a singular pedagogical relation, that is to create, to shape and to reflect is only possible on the ground of the "discovery of childhood" in the 17th/18th Century.[113] Thus, a very specific idea of childhood determines the pedagogical thinking and acting of today. To this idea a normatively coined culture of feelings is connected. In this culture the so called "concerned look"[114] at children plays a central role.

---

    educational and didactical situation at hand, when the claim of a child for individual learning support under given conditions cannot be met in a satisfactory or optimal way.

111 Concerning the functions of school see Helmut Fend (1974).
112 Zirfas 2010, p. 59, transl. by A.K.; in German: "Nur dort, wo wir von einer radikalen Unentscheidbarkeit ausgehen können, kann man für den Anderen die Verantwortung übernehmen, die ihm gerecht wird."
113 The distinction of Childhood Studies and Children's Studies and related disciplines is unfolded in footnote 24.
114 In German: der besorgte Blick (cf. Oelkers 1991)

As we are still dealing with the differences between science and the pedagogical practice one has to mention here, that science is also regarded as politically and socially "engaged"[115]. This opinion will be taken up below.

In terms of the pedagogical relation and also in non-pedagogical approaches the pedagogues are regarded as specialists in creating learning situations. In most of the teaching theories, which refer to the paradigm of a "dignity of practice" (see above), and operate with so called "subjective theories", or even with the paradigm of an "excellent teacher" the teacher is in the foreground. As a rule one assumes that pedagogues are responsible for their own interpretations of events in the classroom and for reflecting the decisions and actions that are decisive for a pedagogical situation. However, their *knowledge about what they do* does not presuppose that they can reflect on *how* they do it.

In general, a teacher structures learning contents and processes as well as social interactions in terms of making actions predictable regarding certain social and material criteria as well as such of space and time. Didactical arrangements (explained above as a lesson planning in advance as well as process-accompanying "pedagogy on the threshold") are combined with pedagogical means. In the professional case the didactical arrangements are pedagogically motivated. This can be the case with a planned recourse to the habitualised patterns of thinking and acting that are for instance discussed as rituals and rules: rituals, rules and territories, that is to say routines of acting, rule-oriented habitūs and a regulated use of space, according to Hartmut VON HENTIG (1993), not only dictate a certain kind of practices in special situations. They also help to act pedagogically by reducing the complexity of a situation and by increasing the predictability of the events during the classes.[116] They are supposed not only to support the purposeful and consequent acting of teachers in class; rituals, rules and territories also independently of the actions of the teacher frame and signalize a school culture and the orders of classes. A consistent (pedagogical) framing of the classes by such and other habitualised patterns of orientation and action as well as by reliable structures should support the pedagogical acting and deciding. This makes it possible for a teacher, also under time pressure, to give attention to unexpected events.

Walter HERZOG & Regula VON FELTEN (2001) do not describe routines, regulations and habitualisations in school as positively as VON HENTIG (1993) does. They moreover give rise to the following concern: "Due to evolutional reasons we possess insights that not only allow us to generate intuitive mathematical and physi-

---

115 Cf. BOURDIEU 2002
116 Cf. the recent publications on the "rediscovery" of the rituals in the context of school. Cf. WAGNER-WILLI 2004; WULF et al. 2004.

cal knowledge, but also intuitive didactics."[117] An "intuitive didactics" is based on routinized experiences and knowledge about school and classes (guided by one's own school biography, or by prejudices about school). Previous experience and knowledge are mostly not reflected in terms of their adequacy. Therefore, these routines rather complicate (lifelong) learning in this area instead of facilitating it, if they make it impossible.[118] Also in other statements about teacher education it is pointed out that a well-developed previous, but habitualized knowledge about children, school and classes is rather a hindrance for the professionalization of teachers than a support.

HERZOG & VON FELTEN (2001) call the typified patterns of perception, interpretation and action that are preferred by the teachers "familiarity traps"[119]. A "familiarity trap" is the one-sided interpretation of norms and values on the basis of one's previous experiences. Socio-cultural, gender and age differences and the proceedings of these differences can fall into the background. The pupils may thus suffer from the "familiarity trap" a teacher falls into and may, hereby, be discouraged from learning. The teacher is then not able to fulfill her/his responsibility towards the pupils to support their learning in an optimal way, maybe without having intended it and without being able to reflect it. It becomes clear here that in our view classes in school are decisively determined by so called "tacit"[120] dimensions of pedagogy.

"Tacit" are unspoken, silent, corporal, spatial, material, hidden, barred or alienated dimensions of pedagogy. These are non-discursive practices, diverse forms of non-explicit social interaction and understanding as well as various influences of complex situational contexts on pedagogy. Tacit in school and in classes in school are moreover also interpersonal differences (see above) as well as a diversity of learning processes and activities such as mimetical learning, forms of adapt(at)ion, model learning, modes of attention, the integration of previous experiences, learning as incorporation or representation, etc. As a "hidden curriculum" different modes of authority and personal integrity are latently effective in classes, as well as unconscious didactical techniques and "subjective theories" and the interaction and relation of well-intended and non-intentional actions: Thus, bodily dispositions, habitūs (habitude, hexis, doxa) and hidden methodologies as

---

117 HERZOG & VON FELTEN 2001, p. 20
118 HERZOG & VON FELTEN 2001, p. 20
119 In German: Vertrautheitsfallen. There are also "familiarity traps" in the diverse scientific approaches.
120 Cf. activities of the scientific network on "Tacit Dimensions of Pedagogy": tacitdimensions.wordpress.com.

well as unspoken interpretative approaches to pedagogical questions play a role as tacit dimensions of pedagogy. Besides, there are also forms of foreignness, such as estrangement, alienation, otherness monocultural or intercultural perspectives; also hybrid cultural figures and practices, processes of social in-/exclusion, forms of repression and power as well as such of an education of the feelings. Also "gouvernementality" and "techniques of the self",[121] "overtones" and controversial discourses can be tacitly effective in a pedagogical situation. In a hidden way also institutional/organizational conditions, symbolic spaces, the architecture, the organization of spaces as well as materials and technologies etc. effect classes at school. Socio-economic conditions and factors as well as formal and informal learning settings, forms of social inequality, the virtual and the real as different life-contexts, diverse concepts of time, influences of earlier realities/history, or certain anticipations of the future, performative effects, artistic processes, social dramas, rituals as well as sceneries and (life) styles latently influence the classes in school. Besides that, also diverse unforeseen events, corporal activities (such as e.g. the modulation of the voice), visual and senso-motorical forms of interaction, the constitution and perception of images, meta-actional behavior, action potentials of metaphors, the modes of a linguistic (re)structuring of representations and discursive practices tacitly stimulate even the well-prepared classes that are supposed to be controlled down to the last detail.

Even though directed to lucidity, also science is not free from black-outs and blind spots. The task to investigate the unknown, disguised or opaque aspects of a scientific approach or study is taken in special by the noetic approach, as it will be unfolded below.

The efforts of the pupils are, as a rule, learning efforts, and learning as such "[…] stays invisible, such as the beginning of the learning, its processing and its dramaturgy."[122] Learning processes cannot be objectified like other processes of a work organization.

Within bodily phenomenology, learning is moreover interpreted as a manifold responsive process at the "point zero"[123] of the bodily orientation. Our bodily orientation is a "point zero", as we cannot reflect on our living body, that is to say, we cannot grasp our own liveliness. We never apprehend ourselves as a whole. We always perceive *something*, and it is not possible to distinguish the external things from our perceptions as it is through our senses we perceive them. Perceptions are responsive processes, in which our *own* matters are equally answered as those that

---

121 Cf. FOUCAULT [1982] 1988, [1966] 1970 et al.
122 MEYER-DRAWE 2008, p. 77, transl. by A.K.
123 In German: Nullpunkt, cf. WALDENFELS 1998, p. 22.

are external to us. Learning processes are therefore not traceable in the sense of evidences, unlike their results.[124]

From this point of view one cannot interpret the achievement of a learning goal in the sense of climbing distinct steps built one on the other, so that at their end the desired learning goal and a certain knowledge stock is acheived. Rather, success in learning is part of the directed processes of seeking and exploring. The understanding of learning processes as an understanding of learning contents implies the attainment of knowledge in different contexts. Knowledge can be influenced and modified by these contexts. Learning is a steady process that principally cannot be brought to an end. It is not so much the distinct knowledge and the autonomous subject directed by her/his own will that rules learning. Rather, the skillful dealing with learning contents, with other persons and with the imponderable aspects of learning stand in the foreground.[125] Jean LAVE (1998) and Martin WEINGARDT (2004) point out "testing" as a primary characteristic of learning: because a learner does *not* know, what s/he will know, when s/he has reached a certain learning goal, learning is characterized by plurivalence and openness. Mainly it is the often unreflected, spontaneous insight that makes learning possible. Even the fact that neither the paths nor the objectives of learning can be precisely known from the beginning makes it possible to be open to learning processes. Learning is thus a big challenge.

In their concept of the "negativity of education" Dietrich BENNER & Andrea ENGLISCH (2005) unfold the various (that is to say teleological, scientific, historical-hermeneutic etc.) experiences of negativity that are made in learning and "Bildung", that is to say in educational processes.[126] This negativity is perceived and processed scarcely consciously and cognitively, rather oblivion is to apply here.[127] If the disappointment of expectations and fears (e.g. of failure) play the central role for pupils in school, the teacher is always confronted with the challenge to reduce the frustrations connected to their learning experiences, to support them in coaching them and dealing with their obstructions to learning. Jörg ZIRFAS (2001, p. 59, transl. by A.K.) writes, that "[…] if there is a gift of education, then only in this way that the educator is radically responsible for the educated person", and Jürgen OELKERS (2007, p. 127) assigns the pedagogues to take away "all sorrows" from the children. This can be interpreted in terms of a representative and exemplary coping of the teacher with the unavailable and negative sides of the

---

124 MEYER-DRAWE 2008, p. 193
125 Cf. MEYER-DRAWE 2000
126 Cf. BENNER 2005
127 BENNER 2005, p. 13

learning processes. The teacher thus shows the pupils how to stand learning processes without causing disaster, or experiencing learning as a disaster. In this sense a teacher has to outright reject the social and societal command of the learners.[128]

The underlying pedagogical relationship of trust and dialogue, basing on adult attitude, determination and serenity, urgently needs more attention and further scientific explanation.[129]

The part of the teacher is thus in a certain sense also in a confining way to make the pupils forget their learning. This has, of course, the status of an aim and not that of a reality that is guaranteed by certain actions and judgements, as also the professional aspects of the practitioning of teachers to a great deal *retreat into darkness*[130]. That is to say, the dispositions, habitūs, spontaneous reactions and normative patterns that substantiate the judgments and the actions of the learners cannot be fully grasped.

Neither the performance of learning nor the pedagogical performance, e.g. the creation of a pedagogical relation, nor the initiating of learning processes are a matter of mere control. A lucid intentionality cannot at all be presupposed, especially not in terms of practitioning in the field of education, as it is the case with the program that drives a professionalization of teaching on the basis of standards ahead (see above). In the center of the teaching profession there are, moreover, dilemmata that are unexpectedly appearing in a class, irritations and incalculable events that go along with the well-skilled acting in the field. The relativity of a presentation, the awareness of happenings on the "back-stages"[131] of the classes, the polmorph normativity, the diverse ambiguities and the confrontation of the teaching person with the her/his prejudices (and that of others) play a central role here, that is to say, they always stand in the focus of the teacher. His/her ability to cope with imponderable and tacit dimensions of pedagogy as well as self-restraint and modesty are important success factors of pedagogues in school. Not only by being a model, also by giving the kids the possibility to learn mutual respect and norms in terms of social relationships and persons at hand is the teaching person important. HEID (2013, p. 254) writes: "Adolescents do not have to respect norms and values, instead they learn to respect the dignity and rights of other concrete persons, as well as critically and competently to participate in discourses

---

128 Cf. WINKLER 2006
129 Cf. RÖBE 2014
130 This is alluding to the statement of Käte MEYER-DRAWE (2008, p. 90, transl. by A.K.), that "the how of learning retreats into darkness" (see above).
131 ZINNECKER 1978

in which one argues about the relvance and quality of intersubjectively verifiable opinions."[132]

In reference to Hans JOAS ([1992] 1996) and Walter HERZOG (2005) we can systematize this kind of modesty. JOAS ([1992] 1996) brings forward the following three fundamental philosophical-ethical arguments against the hypostasis of rational thinking as an omnipotent directive instance. As we will see later, these arguments play a central role also in the context of the noetic theory of science. Here, referring to HERZOG (2005), it will be translated into the school context:

1) Human action is only in special cases the result of directed planning. – HERZOG (2005) writes about predictability and planning: "It is impossible to act pedagogically without accepting the constitutive ignorance [of pedagogical knowledge ...]!"[133] This ignorance is neither inability[134] nor akrasia[135] and not infantia or stupidity.[136] Ignorance is meant here in the sense of a conciliatory impartiality as a fundamental understanding, that is to say: "Teachers must be able to analyze the diversity, heterogeneity and variability of the happenings in their classes in order to be able to rapidly recognize the essential conditions of a concrete situation"[137].

2) The possibilities of control by cognitive processes of thinking are restricted. – HERZOG (2005) describes the field of decision-making and acting of teachers as inherently contradictory, thus as a field of tension; pedagogical situations are "antinomous, paradoxical or dilemmatic"[138]. Every day and inevitably, pupils and teachers experience inherently contradictory situations of decision-making, temporary dilemmata or other problems. They have to cope with these contradictions either by solving them in a competent way, or by modifying

---

132 Transl. by A.K.; in German: "Heranwachsende müssen nicht lernen, Normen und Werte zu respektieren, sie könnten stattdessen lernen, konkrete Menschen zu respektieren, sowie kritisch und kompetent an Diskursen zu partizipieren, in denen über die Relevanz und Qualität intersubjektiv prüfbarer Argumente gestritten wird."
133 HERZOG 2005, p. 314, transl. by A.K.
134 Cf. also SETTON 2006. SETTON (2006) develops an understanding of a sensible ability to act, in which the possibility of failure, the inability to act and the creative performance appear as correlates.
135 Akrasia (Ancient Greek. Ἀκρασία) is the weakness of the will, the lack of self control, acting against better knowing. As a philosophical term it was coined by ARISTOTLE.
136 Akrasia and infantia are states of mind and stagnation that can hardly be described as processual in any way (cf. SETTON 2006).
137 HERZOG & VON FELTEN 2001, p. 23, transl. by A.K.
138 HERZOG 1995, p. 40, transl. by A.K.

them. More often inconsistencies are simply to be carried out. At times it can be a very important pedagogical competence even to abandon "control" and to process antinomies, paradoxes and dilemmata, without solving them.[139] In other cases the contrary is to be done.

3) Seen from an ontogenetic perspective, autonomy is, according to JOAS ([1992] 1996), not an original state, but a result of socialization and a culturally guided product of differentiation[140] that has its origin in the symbiosis of parent and child. – HERZOG (2005) points out that the successful dealing with calamities in pedagogical fields does not only presuppose the acceptance of and coping with one's own ignorance. The acting persons also need to distance themselves from their previous knowledge and they have to unlearn what they have learnt before.[141] We already pointed out the negativity in processes of education and learning.

To sum up, broad explicit diagnostical, pedagogical and didactical knowledge is only then helpful, when it is completed by an implicit everyday knowledge.

Such everyday knowledge bases on orientative knowledge and it is "ingenious"[142]. Being "ingenious/finding" is, according to WALDENFELS (2004b), an essential element of our acting, also of the acts of thinking and of speech. It makes it possible for us to grasp a situation in accordance with our practice and our orientative and experimental knowledge, to react on and create it.[143] Being "ingenious/finding" is no mere rational capability, it is moreover mediated by means of our corporeality, it leads to functionally and evidently consistent results.[144] For

---

139 Cf. the hint of STOJANOV 2004.
140 Also other approaches such as structuralistical, system-theoretical, psychoanalytical etc. refer rational thinking to processes and facts that are previous to it and influence thinking in a fundamental, but tacit way.
141 WALDENFELS 2000, p. 178
142 In German: findig
143 Bernhard WALDENFELS writes about being "ingenious/finding" (2004b, p. 49, transl. by A.K.): "[…] perception is connected to the bodily movements. The older term of a kinaesthetics connects perception with bodily movements. The older term of the kinaesthetics gets a new significance if one does not – as again Husserl suggests – understand it as a mere inner perception of a bodily movement, but a perception in movement. This is a being on the move in terms of being ingenious and cannot be reduced to changing the place, but also entails a constitution of sites. By being on the move in terms of being ingenious one can experiment with positions and constellations and strengthen them by feedback. Inventions are placed where the circuit is not closed."
144 Cf. VAN HAAREN, KLEINER & SCHUBERT 2004, p. 7

example, our climbing when adapting to unusual, unfamiliar steps is based on an "ingenious/finding" process, in which our consciousness does not necessarily play a central role. However, being "ingenious/finding" is not only a bodily knowledge; also the ability to invent something as well as rational constructs and insights base on this ability that is mediated by means of our corporeality.

The central aim of a formation of experience in the field of teacher education that is oriented at science is thus the reflection of practices and strategies in school and classes, not only seen from its manifold explicit, but moreover from its tacit perspectives. Looking at it the other way round, research in the field of practical pedagogy is especially committed to the task of investigating its contradictions as well as its framing conditions.[145]

In a first step, the science-theoretical challenges to this can be linked to the decision on the relation of the general and the particular aspects in the field of science.

---

145 In system-theoretical, also discourse-analytical approaches such conditions are especially stressed.

2. The Challenge of a Relation of the General and the Particular in Scientific Thinking and Research

The concept of science differs in theoretical, historical and critical, as well as in philosophical, epistemological and methodological approaches. Also the general relation of theory and (everyday) practice is defined differently in the diverse meta-theories, respectively epistemologies.[146]

In our context especially the fact of a widened concept of knowledge in the empirical approaches in the field of Children's Studies and Pupil Research is striking. The special significance of Children's Studies and Pupil Research for the professional practice in school has already been pointed out. Georg BREIDENSTEIN & Helga KELLE (1999) have worked out this significance in terms of the methods, procedures and methodologies within the Children's Studies and Pupil Research.[147] They focus on qualitative empirical approaches in this field of Social Research.

Children's Studies in general argue that in the context of the traditionally asymmetrical relationships of kids and adults and in the general social relations of power and care adult patterns of behavior, communication and thinking are, as a rule, considered to be rational and competent. In contrast, the behavior and judgments of kids are usually regarded as irrational, ignorant and minor. Therefore, the Children's Studies see their prior task in investigating and reconstructing the theoretical constructs which are today prevalent, as e.g. that of the "idealized communication between adults"[148]. In such constructs the unwritten everyday rules of the communication between adults, still without exception, claim exclusive validity in terms of the scientific logics, ethics and methodology of research in general and even within research on education in special. The ruling "principles of the everyday conversation"[149] between adults presuppose a rationalistic world view as the natural way of looking at things.[150] This world view is a fixed (adult) system of significance, following certain basic rules and referring to a fixed order of norms and values. However, one cannot operate with such a system of significance in the

---

146 This is the case also in Hans-Georg NEUWEG's (2010) systematics, as he refers to epistemological-methodological approaches (cf. cognitivism, constructivism, theory of perception) as distinctive characteristics of the different approaches to teacher education.
147 BREIDENSTEIN & KELLE 1999, p. 111
148 HÜLST 2000, p. 47
149 LAMNEK 1995, p. 64
150 Cf. HÜLST 2000

frame of research *(together) with* children; it is moreover thwarting. Furthermore, Social Sciences are ruled by a non-acceptance of utterings which are characterized by primary processes, unusual metonymies, metaphors, narratively created images and slang.[151] However, such aspects are integral moments of the articulations of kids. Often the adult, also the adult researcher reacts irritated by the narration of an adolescent, because s/he presumes or demands an explicit, informing character.[152] There is thus a strong tendency in Social Research to interpret verbalizations of children as deficient, erroneous and incongruent.

Out of the perspective of a critical Children's Studies thus many practices appear as dubious which are standard and obligatory in scientific research. Virginia MORROW & Martin RICHARDS (1996) pointed out that the paradigm of research in the Social Sciences for formal reasons does not only exclude childlike, but also many other possible forms of expression and forms of living.[153] The postulate of a research that follows the rational paradigm implicates a symbolical power that only appears more clearly in the context of a research with kids than in other fields of research. As a consequence, the demand of "qualitative" Social Research to meet the singularity of each person and research area is unconditionally put to test in the context of a research on children (respectively by the Children's Studies).[154] That is to say, the conventional arsenals of scientific research are not sufficient for this research field. There is a special need for new instruments and approaches. There is thus the possibility to develop a methodology which fits to this central demand of a qualitative empirical research in Social Sciences in a steadily improved way. BREIDENSTEIN & KELLE (1999) trust this task to the ethnographically and phenomenologically oriented empirical approaches in Children's Studies.

It becomes clear that a further explication of the relationship between kids and adults in terms of differences also explains the diverse processes, tensions and conflicts in the diverse fields of practical pedagogy.

Research on the special knowledge and the possibilities of kids to express their own perspectives also contributes to a scientific modeling of the processes of a transformation of theory to practice and vice versa in the framework of school and school lessons. Children's Studies and Pupil Research, which are interested in the perspectives of the child agents, are thus an important, if not even one of the central reference points for a teacher formation that is oriented at the professional practice in the classroom as well as at scientific research. A generalization of the

---

151 HÜLST 2000, p. 47
152 HAUSENDORF 2001, p. 28
153 Cf. ADORNO & HORKHEIMER ([1944] 1988)
154 FRIEBERTSHÄUSER & PRENGEL 2003, p. 11

adult-rational patterns of perception and interpretation connected to a devaluation of other perspectives, as e.g. those of children, as it is common in Social Research, should be avoided.

The challenge to interrelate general and individual perspectives has been described above as a structural moment of practice in school. In the frame of scientific approaches it shows itself in many facets.

In terms of defining the relation of general and individual perspectives in the field of scientific approaches in general one can make use of the current methodological distinction into a deductive (1), an inductive (2), an abductive (3) approach as well as the "tertium datur". In the following way these forms of logical thinking play a role for the scientific view of reality in school:

(1) An induction is the abstracting conclusion from observed phenomena to more general claims, so as to achieve a general term. One concludes from given conditions to the special or individual case. An induction is thus a conclusion from the specific cases to the general. The interpretations are derived from observations and experiences, or from judgements. Especially theory-generating empirical approaches get their insights in the inductive way.

Latterly, a "practicistic teacher education" is coming up, as e.g. Hans-Georg NEUWEG (2010) shows. According to this model, practice-experienced and inductively arguing (so called "excellent") teachers get involved in the (otherwise deductively modeled) phases of teacher education at the university. Theory-generating inductive procedures are then supposed to bridge the hiatus between science and the professional practices.

However, inductively designed experience and judgements are always partial and based on constructions[155] that are rarely free of deductive conclusions. Inductive conclusions can also be blamed for not providing instruments for critically reflecting the relativity and the limits of their validity, e.g. in terms of effective errors.

(2) A deduction is a conclusion from general to specific cases that is to say from given premises to logically compelling consequences. Characteristic of deductive interpretations of the relation of theory and practice in pedagogy is the expectation that one can derive normative rules with a greater or lesser entitlement to general validity from a pedagogical theory. The concepts of "didactics"[156] and "Bildung"[157] were for a long time the important references in Germany: In terms of pedagogy in school, didactics plays the central role. Theoretically introduced by

---

155 HERZOG & VON FELTEN 2001, p. 22
156 In terms of didactics one mostly refers to the "didactical triangle" of teacher, pupil and content (see: HUDSON 1999).
157 VON HUMBOLDT [1836] 1999

COMENIUS ([1657] 1896), didactics is defined as the art of teaching all things to all men; he writes: "Let the main object of this, our didactics, be as follows: to seek and to find a method of instruction by which teachers may teach less, but learners may learn more by which schools may be the scene of less noise, aversion and useless labour, but of more leisure, enjoyment and solid progress; and through which the Christian community may have less darkness, perplexity, and dissension, but on the other hand more light, orderliness, peace, and rest."[158] Pedagogy is here interpreted as reflected practice.

This corresponds to a "practical science"[159], or to a "profession-oriented science"[160]. Seen from a historical point of view, pedagogy, and herewith teacher education, is a so called "delayed discipline"[161]. It did not at first follow the other Social and Natural Sciences, establishing their disciplines as evidence-based sciences at the beginning of the 20th Century by distinguishing themselves from philosophy. A reason for this may be seen in the fact that pedagogical discourses, because of their normative orientation, cannot be distinguished from ideological paradigms. From such paradigms rules for the educational practice are derived deductively. Especially, since the beginning of the 20th Century and more intensely since the 1960s ideologically based pedagogical models have been complemented and even replaced by forms of empirically oriented scientific argumentations and audits.[162] The fundamental thought of scientific empiricism is the inductive achieving of results. Empirical metrical and/or experimental approaches that are verified by certain procedures of testing or evaluation, or even consensus-based insights prefer, as a rule, hypothesis-based, that is to say deductive evidence. Strict affordances to scientific procedures, as e.g. the investigations on the basis of "representative" samples and the hypothesis- and method-based quantitative analysis of method-based collected data with the claim of objectivity will make it possible to derive deductive conclusions from the results of research.

---

158 COMENIUS [1657] 1896, preface
159 Cf. BAUMER & ROEDER 1994, p. 41
160 HERZOG 2005
161 TENORTH 1989, p. 118 ff.
162 Cf. the historical introduction of the Educational Sciences as a discipline at university has been driven forward decisively by Peter PETERSEN (1884–1952). – ĶESTERE & OZOLA (2011, p. 306) write about the Europen context: "The history of educational institutions is a widely studied issue, while the history of pedagogy as a scientific discipline has attracted the attention of the researchers only since the late 1990s, and it still remains an insufficiently studied issue both in the Baltic States and elsewhere in Europe. [...] Germany has always been the leader among European countries with regard to the development of pedagogy as a scientific discipline."

Cybernetical, governmental, or system-theoretical as well as technologically oriented approaches e.g. start from the assumption of the possibility of a hypothesis-based, that is to say scientific-deductive definition of the conditions of school practice. Furthermore, the theoretical underpinning of professional practices, as e.g. Robert Faux (2000) presents it, is deductively constructed.

(3) Abduction is, according to Charles S. Peirce ([1903] 1934, CP 5.171), the "[…] only logical operation which introduces any new idea".[163] An abductive conclusion is a so called "original argument". By means of the abductive method insights that expand the already existing stock of knowledge as well as synthetical statements are possible. The point about the concept of abduction, according to Peirce ([1903] 1934), is that an instinctive, pre-theoretical moment of insight is combined with a procedural, methodical-rational forwarding of hypotheses. An abductive assumption is described as a "capacity of insight", or "flash of insight"; "[…] it is the idea of putting together what we had never before dreamed of putting together which flashes the new suggestion before our contemplation".[164] An abductive conclusion is initiated by a fact requiring explanation that enters into the interpreter's horizon of experiences and expectations. In the sense of a de-

---

163 One can find a similar argument in Johann Friedrich Herbart's texts (1837, p. 19, transl. by A.K.), as he writes: "Logic gives the most general regulations for identifying terms, to structure and to connect them. It is the indispensable propedeutics for all of the […] sciences […]; logic presupposes concepts as already known; and it does not care about the specific content of them. Therefore, it is actually not an instrument of scientific discovery striving for the investigation of something new, but for the guidance in presenting what one already knows." In German: "Die Logik giebt die allgemeinsten Vorschriften, Begriffe zu sondern, zu ordnen, und zu verbinden. Sie ist die nothwendige Vorschule für sämtliche […] Wissenschaften […] Die Logik setzt die Begriffe als bekannt voraus; und bekümmert sich nicht um den eigenthümlichen Inhalt eines jeden derselben. Daher ist sie nicht eigentlich ein Werkzeug der Untersuchung, wo etwas Neues gefunden werden soll, sondern eine Anleitung zum Vortrage dessen, was man schon weiß."

164 Peirce [1903] 1934, CP 5.181. According to Karl R. Popper (1992, p. 58) there is no instant rationality nor are there singly decisive "crucial experiments", but only "crucial falsifying experiments". There is no logical, rationally reconstructable way to discover something new. Popper (1992, p. 8) assumes a "creative intuition" (cf. Henri Bergson), which he describes as not rational and methodically incomprehensible. Popper (1992, p. 8) also shares Albert Einstein's opinion: In "[…] the 'search for those universal laws […] from which a picture of the world can be obtained by pure deduction, there is no logical path', he [Einstein] says, 'leading to these […]. They can only be reached by intuition, based upon something like an intellectual love [in German: Einfühlung] of the objects of experience.'"

monstrative logics (*if A, then C*) a missing element is inserted in a playful and experimental way, until a plausible solution is found. The "eureka" that is brought up in such a *free play* of the imagination and such an inferential process may even initiate a new (habit of) thought. An abductive conclusion is not at all arbitrary, as Peirce ([1903] 1934) points out, but it gives a plausible explanation for the things that have to be clarified: "The surprising fact, C, is observed. But if A were true, C would be a matter of course. Hence, there is reason to suspect that *A* is true."[165] Abductive logics is a pragmatic strategy with the aim (or a subconscious decision with that effect) of a minimisation of the ever consistent risk of error.

According to Uwe Wirth (2001) human capabilities in general can be described as abductive proceedings, because they are ruled by "perceptive judgments"[166] as original creative acts. The perception processes that found specific schemes of reasoning, cognition and action are based on social practices.[167]

The abduction grants access to new knowledge.[168] Therefore, the logical operation of abduction is not only important for scientific research. It also plays a central role in approaches to instruction and in the analysis of processes and practices in a teaching-learning-situation.

(4) Klaus Heinrich (1981) challenges the binary logic with his term "tertium datur". He places the "tertium datur" in the form of a "tertium comparationis" at the basis of all events, by writing: in every decision or statement "[…] the counterpart and the *in* never disappears"[169]. "Indeed I must separate, otherwise I do not have a subject. But for the sake of the subject, I revoke the separation in the judgment that fixes it and unifies it with the judge at the same time"[170]. The "tertium datur" does not question the consistency or the conclusiveness of a cause; it merely describes both, non-existence and an existence at the same time; negativities are viewed as modifications of a positive reality rather than as their logical opposite. For example, a "tertium datur" is given, if antinomies, i.e. controversial statements or circumstances, are viewed as equally well founded or proven (in the case of formal systems).

The "tertium datur" can be interpreted praxeologically, epistemologically as well as methodologically. With the concept of "tertium datur" it is possible to explain as a quality what is perceived as undefined, unplannable and spontaneous

---

165 Peirce [1903] 1934, CP 5.189
166 Peirce [1903] 1934, CP 5.192
167 Cf. Reichertz 2003, transl. by A.K.
168 On problems with Peirce's concept of abduction see Hoffmann 1999.
169 Heinrich 1985, p. 16, transl. by A.K.
170 Heinrich 1985, p. 15 f., transl. by A.K.

about the teaching profession; at the same time one can epistemologically define the logics of teaching in more detail.[171]

Epistemological concepts of science make use of all kinds of logical closing. In the following, the noetic perception of science is discussed in dissociation from the (much more popular and well-known) noematic perception of science. Hereby, it should be kept in mind that the differentiation of these two concepts of science is principally of an ideal type nature. The two perspectives can also appear with different emphasis in one and the same setting at the same time. The following description is based on the fact that the epistemological difference between the two epistemological approaches is sustained in pedagogical practice.

2.1 The Phenomenological Noematic and the Noetic Concept of Science as a Basis for Modeling Teacher Education

The epistemological differentiation between so-called "noeses" and "noemata" goes back to Edmund HUSSERL ([1913] 1983). Noeses define thetic actions by which the noemata are constituted as "given". This means that what is given (for us) is perceived as the result of defining thetic actions – according to HUSSERL ([1913] 1983) these are "intentions"; noeses constitute a subject in its modalities of existence as a meaningful suchness[172] (noema), and thus as a variable subject of the external world. HUSSERL ([1913] 1983) emphasizes that in striving for new (scientific) knowledge, the (supposedly) real content of something "given" must be placed in parentheses. This methodic step (epoché) is supposed to open the view on the noeses. – We will come back to the "phenomenological method".

Based on this differentiation between noeses and noemata, Alwin DIEMER (1964) differentiates between a "noetic" and a "noematic" concept of science. The noematic concept of science aims for the given things (noemata). Meanwhile, the noetic concept assumes that the act of creating meaning is detectable in the form of a noesis.[173] While the noematic concept of science thus refers to that which is given (for us) and has the factual and accordingly the "positive" as its source and legitimation, the noetic concept of science examines the laws of constitution and the genetic aspects of scientific research as well as of everyday reality.

This impulse will be pursued and elaborated further in the following by taking the postulation of an "end of grand narratives"[174] into account. The postulation is a

---

171 Cf. KRAUS 2002
172 In German: Sosein
173 Cf. HUSSERL [1913] 1983, p. 205 f.
174 LYOTARD ([1979] 1984), see above.

critique of the institutional and ideological forms of knowledge. It is flanked with other reflexive positions toward science and it partly corresponds with them.[175] In general, a hypothesis-testing, also metrizing quantitative (social) research is differentiated in an ideal type of research from a hypothesis-*generating, reconstructive*, qualitative (social) one. However, most of the metricating quantitative approaches as well as those, which are considered part of qualitative research are classified as noematic in our model. The majority of qualitative approaches are considered as noetic approaches with noematic aspects. The differentiation by Gaston BACHELARD ([1938] 2004) between the "positivist" and the "epistemological" approach to science is also common.[176] As for the differentiation between qualitative and quantitative research, the differentiation between "positivist" and "epistemological" sciences is hereby considered, although it is not taken as the basis for argumentation.[177]

---

175 Here, one can name among many other thinkers Friedrich NIETZSCHE (1844–1900), Edmund HUSSERL (1859–1938), Theodor W. ADORNO (1903–1969), Paul FEYERABEND (1924–1994). All these scientists have their own science critical standpoints. Also diverse activist movements, such as in the 1960s the "Radical Science Movement" and the Student Movement, the Second Women and the Ecology Movement as well as the Post-Colonial Critique of Science, have assumed science-theoretical and -critical positions.

176 Epistemology (from the Ancient Greek ἐπιστήμη knowledge, sciences, true knowledge and λόγος lógos word, speech, teaching) is a branch of philosophy that deals with the teaching of knowledge and science. In the 1930ies Gaston BACHELARD (1971) introduced the distinction between epistemology and knowledge theory in order to examine the problems of science with the explicit exclusion of "traditional" philosophical and ideological assumptions. His "épistémologie" is considered as "a new type of philosophy" and as the "self-consciousness" of science, which BACHELARD (1971) confronts with the logical neo-positivism of his time.

177 BACHELARD (1971) links objectivity to the conditions of objectivation and considers them as mainly the psychological problem of overcoming one's subjectivity. He refers structural blockades against scientific thinking to the immediacy and to the affective strength of subjective experience. By interpreting objectivity as a pedagogical challenge, he puts the fact into light that the scientific mind is the result of a "formation". The philosopher represents thus a rather exclusive understanding of knowledge and science. He regards a scientific experience as contrary to the usual experience. His concept of an "epistemological rupture" (*coupure épistémologique*) asserts the strict separation between everyday/natural and scientific experience. "Epistemological ruptures" take place when epistemological obstacles are defeated. It is when an epistemological obstacle is met, that the ways of thinking that prevent progress in terms of immanent und (yet) unreflected structures become visible, not only causing a more precise knowledge, but also a restructuration of the scientific mind. BACHELARD also assumes

In the following, the distinction in a noetic and a noematic concept of science is further unfolded. Subsequently, differences and similarities between the two scientific approaches are presented with respect to their relationship to the orientative and practical knowledge of teachers. The challenge profile of the professionality of a teacher is an important point of reference, namely investigating teaching in terms of a typology of triggering concomitant learning processes by means of different knowledge formats.

---

the necessity of an explicit initiative to participate in the scientific thinking; a "scientific spirit" could, according to the French epistemologist, only form completely if by virtue of a cognitive-affective regulation of the psyche and in terms of a "progressive rationalization". The processes that lead to this abstraction are, according to the French philosopher, intimately linked to inventivity and imagination, which emancipate us from the *jail of sensitivity*: "It is often said that imagination is the ability of forming images. But it is rather the ability of deforming images given by perception, and it is especially the aptitude of *freeing us from the first images, of changing images*". In French: "On veut toujours que l'imagination soit la faculté de former des images. Or elle est plutôt la faculté de déformer les images fournies par la perception, elle est surtout la faculté de nous *libérer des images premières, de changer les images*" (BACHELARD [1943] 1990, p. 7 f.). The spirit makes explorations beyond the perception of real space. It is self-willed, which detaches the self-willed from the immediate experience and which even stands in open contradiction to the primary reality. BACHELARD ([1957] 1998, p. 186) regards the primary reality as messy and formless, and he attributes an optimally high degree of objectivity to the scientificalness which he targets. In *La formation de l'esprit scientifique* primary reality is described as the pre-scientific state of mind: "[…] On ne se détache pas du merveilleux quand une fois on lui a donné sa créance, et pendant longtemps on s'acharne à rationaliser la merveille plutôt qu'à la réduire." (BACHELARD [1938] 2004 p. 131; in English: "one does not detach oneself from the marvelous once one has given it credibility, and the tendency of rationalising the marvelous rather than reducing it is long-lasting"). Furthermore, he uses a historical analysis of science, by focusing its failures. The researchers of the 18th Century he addresses as infantilized as he attributes already the "concrete step" within his "three-stage law for the scientific spirit" to the "infantile or sophisticated mind", which is dominated by "naive curiosity" (BACHELARD [1938] 2004, p. 23). – In addition to the dubious and unscientific imagery (e.g. "retarded sciences") the devaluation of the "childlike" is of course not permissible in our context. However, his epistemological approach, that also e.g. Thomas S. KUHN (1962) in his "paradigm-approach" used, is of science-theoretical importance and it also underlies the logics of a "noetic" and a "noematic" scientific approach.

2.2 On the Noematic Concept of Science

According to the, nowadays widely accepted, result-oriented noematic concept of science, universally valid statements about (e.g. social) realities are sought, whereas no normative statements and comments should be made. Science is rather taken to be (the only) guarantor for value-neutral, representative, reliable, valid and objective statements. A documentation of results, or the confirmation that a theory can be generalized, i.e. that its application to certain facts is valid, reliable and objective, is regarded as guaranteed by a scientifically verified and strictly controlled methodical approach. The noematic idea of the empirical research within the Humanities and the Social Sciences is oriented toward a notion of experience similar to the experimental sciences and occasionally follows metric laws. According to the noematic concept, scientifically generated theoretical knowledge is taken to be principally applicable to scientifically defined circumstances. It is regarded being independent of concrete decisions, practices and their conditions.[178] The development of science is seen as an immanent progress. In the case of education, the universal validity of scientific, empirically proven and theoretical statements is differentiated from educational and teaching practices, from the volatility of a particular condition field of judgment and action, and from the subjective approaches of the agents.[179] In the noematic concept, the terms uniqueness and universality thus mark the separating line between science and everyday life, also education in general and educational and teaching practices in special.

Also so-called qualitative, for example, objective hermeneutic approaches[180], or the qualitative content analysis[181] regard their scientific interpretations as "positive", or "secured" and "objective", respectively they believe in the possibility of such objectivity. Generality is claimed here for a final, conclusive consensus of a scientific result.

Historically, the Natural and Social Sciences use the noematic claim to digress further from philosophical approaches for truth, which they accuse of speculation, subjectivism and normativity. In contrary, empirical research results are understood as scientifically *reliable* and *evident knowledge.*

A noematically-oriented science within the educational fields provides data which serve as a basis for primarily structural decisions in a context of educational policy or school organization. Thus, especially the scientific results to which

---

178 Cf. RYLE ([1949] 1963, p. 35
179 Cf. the systematics of concepts on teacher education by NEUWEG (2010).
180 OEVERMANN 2000
181 MAYRING 2003

educational policy currently refers and projects concerned with quality-assurance and -development in the education sector are mostly evidence-based. However, to record teaching and learning practices by the noematic approach means an extrapolation.

Nowadays there is an extensive noematic research on expert knowledge of teachers and on formal learning, especially regarding its results. The question to which extent generalized and numerically redacted knowledge, which has been generated under scientific standards, can be used for a planned educational practice is discussed controversially in the frame of the noematic concept of science. Besides critical scientific positions in this respect,[182] nowadays a high practical relevance in the educational field is attributed to noematic scientific theories and results.

This is, for example, claimed for cybernetic, governmental and system-theoretical contexts and for macro- and especially micro-systemic models of control[183] derived from these approaches. According to the "governmental theory"[184], e.g. in connection with the "new public management"-approach[185], the structure and

---

[182] Fritz OSER (1997b, p. 226) has a leading role in the sense of a noematic perspective on teacher education. However, in drawing up its standards, he points to the difficulties in predicting the reliability of standardized performance surveys and warns of a "means-purpose superstition"; he writes: "However, it can be said also of the pedagogical practitioners that they cannot meet adequately the 'requirement of the individual case', because the maneuver is limited." Cf. already HERBART 1969 [1802], p. 285

[183] VON SALDERN 2010, p. 61 f.

[184] "Governmental theories", simply "governance" Latin gubernare; synonymous with Ancient Greek κυβερνάω: lead the rudder; see also "cybernetics".

[185] "New Public Management", formally conceptualized by HOOD (1991), is intended to produce a lean and efficient public system, where executive leaders evolve general strategies, while the selection of means and the organization of practice are assigned to subordinate managers and ordinary civil servants, who are supposed to be controlled, scrutinized, rewarded, or punished according to the results they obtain. The agenda of "New Public Management" covers public reforms that are focused on increased efficiency, more competition, a reorganization that moves subordinate units away from the executive level, and the fragmentation of organizational units and tasks. Other features include the use of private-sector management techniques, a greater emphasis on results, and increased customer-orientation. Since the 1980s this model has continued to be influential all over the world for two decades, but has peaked in some Anglo-Saxon countries during recent years. Although the concept of governance and that of New Public Management originated from two different sets of concerns and theoretically are quite different, both perspectives have incorporated each other's ideas. The governance literature has e.g. embraced the ideas of performance indicators. (Cf. KLIJN 2012)

process organization of public institutions can be systematically determined and improved according to the principles of accountability, responsibility and transparency. "The normative use of governance is based on the assumption that the increased use of new control modes increases efficiency and effectiveness and generally allows the government to recover its capacity to act."[186]

2.2.1 Criticism of Noematic Models of Teacher Education

The claim which is occasionally advocated in the noematic research approach (though not to structure practices) to formulate general guidelines and specifications (e.g. performance expectations) for the educational practice is questioned from within its own ranks.[187] Therefore, noematically-oriented studies, such as those that have been carried out under auspices like *"Teachers matter!"*[188], arrive at summaries such as the following: "[…] to obtain a resilient statement in view of the complicated mesh of active factors that contribute to learning gains is methodologically extremely difficult."[189]

In the following, the concepts of competence development, standardization and "subjective theories", which are considered noematic and are commonly used in the field of teaching and education, are highlighted and subjected to criticism. They have in common that they target the development of (a special kind of) critical thinking as a "[…] key component and guiding concept of professionalism."[190] These concepts are neither interpreted uniformly, nor can they be distinguished significantly from each other. In the following, only the currently relevant definitions of these concepts are presented.[191]

The term "governance" describes a decision-making process and indicates the formal and informal arrangements that include external governance, which refers to relations between individual institutions and their supervisors, and internal governance, which refers to lines of authority within institutions. Governance overlaps considerably with management; the latter is seen as the implementation and execution of policies. Also formal governance is official and explicit, while informal governance refers to the unwritten rules that govern how people relate to each other.

186 VON BLUMENTHAL 2005, p. 1163, transl. by A.K.
187 See footnote 172
188 Cf. e.g. www.oecd.org/education/school/attractingdevelopingandretainingeffective teachers-finalreportteachersmatter.htm [latest access: 10.03.2015]
189 TERHART 2007, p. 215, transl. by A.K.
190 STEINER 2004, p. 239, transl. by A.K.
191 The potentials for teacher education of the concepts described here as noematically will fall behind; this is accepted in view of the harsh critique on them.

2.2.1.1 Teacher Education as a Development of "Competences"

Today, concepts on education primarily refer to the action- and application-oriented concept of competence as well as to the notion of a competence-based professionalism, which holds a key position in school and in teacher formation. There are different defintions of competence.[192]

The cognitivist perception, according to which competences are defined as cognitions, is widely seen as decisive for the concept of competence. According to the approach of Cognitive Psychology competence development is considered as the construction of complex person-related, social, professional, in the case of teacher education e.g. didactic-pedagogical, and situation-specific operational schemes. In cognitive concepts the interpretations of a situation and the possibilities for action are put in relation. The competence development is particularly linked to the assumption of accountability as well as to the attribution of responsibilities and to application situations. According to WEINERT (2001)[193], competences are based on skills that, through responsible action (practice, transfer, application, etc.), are developed to capabilities and then to competences. The orientation toward specifically given requirements is regarded as central to the acquisition of competences.

Andreas FREY (2006) illustrated the action-oriented development of competences in a diagram, in which activities are portrayed by reflection loops (arrows in the diagram):

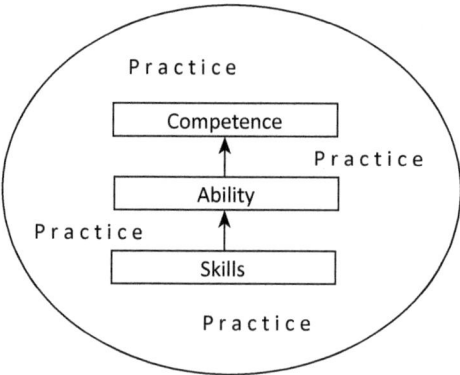

Fig. 1   Source: FREY 2006, p. 32

---

192 As mentioned above, in this essay the definition of Jürgen LÖWISCH (2000) is preferred.
193 WEINERT's definition of "competences" plays a central role for German curricula as well as for the general idea about Bildung.

WEINERT (2001, p. 51) writes: "Action competence comprehensively combines those intellectual abilities, content-specific knowledge, cognitive skills, domain-specific strategies, routines and subroutines, motivational tendencies, volitional control systems, personal value orientations, and social behaviors into a complex system [that] specifies the prerequisites required to fulfill the demands of a particular professional position, of a social role, or a social project."[194] In school, motivational, volitional and social dispositions should be regarded from the standpoint of social (e.g. school) success and as connected to the stock of school knowledge. It is assumed that competences are on one hand based on the capacity to act and on the knowledge of individuals. On the other hand, competences also define the opportunities of a personal development. Competences are reality-proven coping capabilities of individuals. At the same time competences function as an implicit argument structure, within which success and problem solving are not conceived from the perspective of the individuals, but from that of a society in change. Disembedding from traditional social forms and commitments of the industrial society (e.g. class, family, institutions of the welfare state), society turns towards an increasing ascription of control and responsibility to the individual.[195] "Individualisation" is interpreted as the ability of self-responsibility, -control, -motivation, -management and self-marketing. A competence development is thus not limited to (practical) knowledge in a technical discipline. It is also a measure to assess a personality structure that is capable or incapable of coping with (social) requirements at hand, and personality is required to develop according to predetermined and fixed expectations.

Eckart LIEBAU (2003) critisizes the intricate twofold nature of this competence concept: "Competence is the result of competence – you become capable when you become responsible, i.e. accountable"[196]. The concept of competence thus comprises a profile of capabilities, which in terms of the competence development has always been presupposed. A person thus possesses the competence to perform a task, or to solve a problem, if the requirements of the situation coincide with her/his individual abilities. Here, the (still) developing subjectivity takes a backseat behind the (externally presented, social) requirements that have to be fulfilled competently. To follow LIEBAU (2003), with the development of competences – in a twofold rejection of the individual – the social overlay of a personality structure is described and linked to the demand for adaptation of the individual. The (common) interpretation of the competence development as a process of "Bildung"

---

194 Cf. also OECD 2001
195 Cf. ACHATZ & TIPPELT 2001
196 LIEBAU 2003, p. 424, transl. by A.K.

thus forbids itself. – Not least the motivations and social dispositions of pupils are not necessarily aligned with school knowledge and instruction.

However, on one hand the development of competences is handed over to the learning subjects and to their self-learning, or self-education. On the other hand, it is expected from the teacher. In both respects, neither the individual learning development and (self-)education, nor the pedagogical relationship is placed at the center. The sole aim, according to LIEBAU (2003), is the mere adaptation of the individual to the demands of society. The cognitivist interpretation of the concept of competence is critisized of bringing an exaggeration of dull strategic thinking and an overemphasis of calculation to all areas of life, for which it claims validity.[197] Correspondingly, the psychometric modeling of competences and the idea of a measureable output of a competence development is criticized of the suppression of unconcious, unverbalizable and not measurable aspects of learning and knowledge going along with it.

In the context of teacher education and school the development of competences is sometimes reduced to a teacher training with a minimum of theoretical implications. The criticism of the concept of competence of being oriented to efficiency and competition models far from all other educational orientations corresponds in parts with the allegation brought toward the rationalistic concept of "Bildung".[198]

As already mentioned before, education and schools are justified by the neo-humanistic concept of "Bildung", which regards itself as a personality development, led by the idea of emancipation, as well as a mode of assumption of social responsibility. This is especially the case when it comes to the ability of an independent judgement and responsible decision that lies beyond the acquisition of practical knowledge. The concept of "Bildung" is therefore a key point of reference for models of school learning. Although, due to the qualifying, allocating and selecting social functions of school, it is only valid to a limited extent.[199] However,

---

197 In 2006, the Priority Program (SPP) 1293 of the DFG "Competence Models for Assessing Individual Learning Outcomes and Evaluating Educational Processes" was established, from which a further clarification on this issue from the noematic view could be worked out. SCHOTT & GHANBARI (2008), for example, are not oriented on didactic task descriptions for their competence structure model.
198 Thus, for example, the education and (cognitivist) competence concept that underlies the widely reviewed and education politically highly relevant PISA-tests, has been questioned from different sides. The science-based criticism of the PISA studies relates to methodological, methodical and procedural aspects. (Cf. for example JAHNKE & MEYERHÖFER 2006)
199 See above and KRAUS 2010.

the concept of "Bildung" is accused of suggesting its interpretation as a purely self-serving (self-) preparation for the requirements of the labor market in terms of a self-centered improvement of one's own life chances.[200] The dimensions of education processes that are oriented at a personal, (inter-)cultural and social development as well as at collective social ideas and responsibilities are underexposed as a whole. Furthermore, it is argued that the concept of "Bildung" is contradictory and, because of difficulties in its operationalization as well as due to its inflationary use, has even been undermined, based on historical disavowal. The concept of "Bildung" is further accused of being inconclusive concerning the success of teaching, or the individual learning processes.

However, this also applies to the now circulating ideal-typical models of competence and the criteria for a conducive learning as well as for its empirical verification.[201]

In particular, it is scientifically unclear whether a competence-based teacher education is purposeful at all: "Neither the hope of being able to determine the necessary competences for the teaching profession skills empirically, nor the hope that the corresponding training programs have met the expectations has been fulfilled. The provision of training programs is ultimately [not more than] a normative act."[202] There is thus a need to work on the potentials of the competence concepts, seen e.g. by Maike ADEN & Maria PETERS (2012).

2.2.1.2 Standards, Standardized Teaching and Teacher Education

In Germany, especially the model for a standardized teacher education by OSER and colleagues has shown wide-spread effect: according to Jürgen OELKERS & Fritz OSER (2001) "standards" are necessary professional instructional competences that are (or can be) applied in diverse and complex situations; OSER (1997a, p. 27f., transl. by A.K.) defines standards as follows: "We believe that standards are perfectly executed or perfectly mastered. Standards are in many situations applicable competences and capabilities which can be used only by professionals, but not by laymen or by persons of other professions. Knowledge of professional relevance is composed of complex knowledge structures overarching specialized knowledge. We consider standards to be stocks of knowledge that must be acquired in an absolutely necessary form, complying with an action-oriented degree of quality. [...] Only experts dispose of standards, and as for that a layman without

---

200 Cf. MASSCHELEIN & RICKEN 2003
201 Cf. EDER & ALTRICHTER 2009, p. 306f.
202 CRIBLEZ 2003, p. 332, transl. by A.K.

any precondition can produce the same results as a professional, thus one cannot here speak of standards. Standards are marked both by performance and quality levels, on the other hand they can also be a guide for the professional training and for its evaluation." Standards are perfectly executed as well as optimally controlled abilities and skills that are applicable in many situations. They are supposed to be compatible with pedagogical theory and practice. Standards are also deemed to be proven in their feasibility.

Standards, in particular standards of education are considered as the central elements of control in educational planning today.[203] The efforts of a standardization in terms of school performance and aptitude tests for the selection of teacher students, or teachers in service gain ever more ground. The circulating standard lists (OSER, KMK 2004, etc.) are actually used as the basis for various governmental strategies and papers, such as for the study programs (e.g. module handbooks) in the field of teacher education.

With respect to teacher education, professional standards are supposed to counteract the widespread and empirically raised accusation of its arbitrariness and superficiality.[204] Relevant to the recent introduction of standards for the teacher profession were studies on personality profiles of teachers, such as that conducted by Johannes MAYR & Angelika PASEKA (2002), who have shown that introversion, strong neurotic tendencies and a low degree of self-control of teachers have a negative impact on the quality of their teaching and their job satisfaction. Inventories for a personality description and investigation of teachers, developed in response to the publication of the results of such studies, are now regarded to be accessible by means of psychometric models of competence and assessment methods. From the viewpoint of their standardization, competences are not understood as being static like personality traits, but moreover, and this is only hypothetical, as developable. Relevant (psychometric) instruction competences, which are transformed to quality or development stages, are then placed in relation to the course and duration of personality training and they are investigated for the sake of a standardized capacity building.

---

203 WACKER et al. 2012
204 OELKERS & OSER 2001

2.2.1.3 Teacher Education as a Development of "Subjective Theories" and the Concept of "Reflective Practitioning"

"Subjective theories" (STs) are qualified as complex cognitive systems reflected in an explicit argumentation in which the view of a subject manifests itself.[205] The approach to teacher education emanating from the STs of professional teachers is interpreted in terms of the professional practice for which it aims to prepare.

Here, professionalism is basically considered in terms of the epistemological subject model, which is oriented to language and communication capabilities, reflexivity and rationality.[206] What is constitutive of actions is supposed to be represented in the consciousness of the agents; the subject is constituted by its own capabilities of instruction and (positive) opportunities of development.[207] The STs of teachers concerning school, pupils, schooling and interactive processes are supposed to correspond at least in structure to scientific theories.[208]

Teacher education which involves instruction-guiding STs in the teaching practice aims to match them with scientific theories and results.[209] The investigation of STs is usually carried out in the mode of "thinking aloud" as a subsequent, or even instruction-concomitant verbalization of everyday school and teaching situations, such as teaching-learning processes and problem-solving approaches. Likewise, STs are investigated e.g. in guided interviews as retrospective reports on actions of the own, using the structure-laying technique by self-confrontation interviews, or in the video-graphically-aided subsequent confrontation of a teacher with her/his class instruction.

STs are considered an adequate object of teacher education during all of its phases. However, the following problems are associated with this concept:

1. It is simply taken for granted that the social conditions and actions which are relevant to the teacher profession can be represented adequately in instruction-related (self-) statements;[210]
2. The idea that STs can be detected in the methodologically-based consensual feedback and in an "objective", i.e. scientifically-based approach is purely hypothetical;

---

205 GROEBEN 1988
206 Cf. GROEBEN et al. 1988
207 GROEBEN 1988
208 Cf. e.g. GROEBEN & SCHEELE 1982 and SCHEIRING 1998.
209 Cf. GROEBEN & SCHEELE 1982
210 BREUER 1995, p. 161

3. STs as a part of teacher education suggests putative therapeutic actions.[211] However, these do not follow any method and are thus "wild", not reported, not skilled and unpredictable in their consequences.
4. STs as everyday concepts of individuals, which are not necessarily shared intersubjectively, stand in a close relation to the individual experience. They substantiate the self-confidence and the implicit self-efficacy expectations of a person and are thus part of her/his inviolable integrity[212].
5. A critique of the STs of a teacher will eventually put the dignity of his/her professional practice and his/her professionalism in question.
6. As a "familiarity trap" (see above) STs may hamper a professional self-admitting to the diverse intra- and interpersonal as well as cultural differences and tensions in the educational work field, or even make it impossible.
7. The development of an individualized didactics, which reflects the fact that individual STs should be tested in ever-changing practical contexts and possibly be modified is still a desideratum of research.

The testing of STs of teacher trainees and teachers in service, as it is currently done on a large scale under the sign of "excellent teacher", the "good school" and in an evaluative way, thus appears to be questionable. Instead, the aim should be to maintain the dignity of pedagogical instruction in the sense of understanding the STs of the teachers (as well as those of the teacher students) in terms of their constant change and development.

Attention can be drawn here to the concept of a "reflective practitioner" by Donald SCHÖN (1983), which is internationally a very important reference. While this is not the place to reflect all facets of his differentiated and well-developed concept, we will concentrate on its core idea.

Defined as a critique of a technologically reduced profession theory, it is argued that theoretical contents cannot be directly applied to professional practice. As also BÖHLE et al. (2004) emphasize (see above), SCHÖN (1983) stresses that professionality in general includes the ability to adequately perceive imponderable situations in daily professional life and to deal with them appropriately. Referring to Michael POLANYI's (1966) concept of "implicit knowing" and Gilbert A. RYLE's ([1949] 1963) concept of a "knowing how", SCHÖN (1983) thus defines this ability as a reflectivity within professional practitioning; he speaks of "reflection-in-action": "Reflection-in-action has a critical function [...]. Reflection gives rise to on-the-

---

211 GROEBEN 1988
212 Under certain circumstances it may be necessary to put aside the value of personal integrity with the requirements for professional action.

spot experiment. We think up and try out new actions intended to explore the newly observed phenomena, test our tentative understandings of them, or affirm the moves we have invented to change things for the better."[213]

Even if the signature of this concept aims at a critique of rationalist approaches, the idea of a practice-oriented reflexive teacher education falls back to "subjective theories", as tentative "reflective practitioning" is supposed to be followed up and educated by "reflective teaching" and a supervised reflection of one's own lessons.

"Familiarity traps" that hamper "subjective theories" and "reflective teaching" turn out as a big challenge. The aim should, therefore, be to look for possibilities to detect these "familiarity traps" in the STs of the actors. However, it must be considered that the fact that "familiarity traps" present themselves in particular for trainees and teachers is not surprising, given the great importance of the uncertainties in their professional workfield. Relying on the familiar within the scope of professional practice is even a central aspect of the dignity of their professional practice (see above). "Familiarity traps" should, therefore, not in the noematic sense be negotiated as research results. We will come back to this point.

What should have been evident here is that noematic thinking emanates (perhaps without intending this, in any case without considering it extensively) from several epistemological axioms that imply narrowness. While these fixations may appear unproblematic in relation to many research subjects, they are in any case not suitable for the description of educational and teaching processes and practices, of educational relationships and interactions nor for the modeling of a related (noetic) professional*ization* (instead of professional*ism*) related to them.

2.2.1.4 Criticism of the Noematic Concept of Science in Education and Outlook on the Phenomenological Noetic Alternative

The noematic view of science received widespread criticism in the 1980s. Among other things this is due to the fact that an increasing variety of unpredictable factors of human existence have become clear, from the perspective of risk research as well as in concepts of Social Sciences and Humanities, over the past decades. It has been found that during the primarily technologically based (and resting on scientific results) transformation of the world by mankind many calamities are created that cannot be overcome by a natural way. The incidental and hazardous potentials of civilizational developments can obviously not be overcome simply technologically; taking responsibility is in demand.

---

213 SCHÖN 1983, p. 23

Further, companies are nowadays subject to rapid changes in the social context that lead to far-reaching instabilities and uncertainties. Social changes are described, for example, as a pluralization of lifestyles that will soon include all cultural practices and areas, breaking with the traditions. At the same time, as the consequence of an increasing globalization, there is a generalization, homogenisation and virtualization of human life scopes.

Pronounced heterogeneous starting points for learning arise from such developments, constantly challenging educational advantages and disadvantages and, last but not least, unsecured future prospects, especially in ecological, economic and social terms for more or less all social groups.

Viewed for the entire society, there is also a growing uncertainty with respect to institutional, political, economic and social responsibilities and accountabilities. Given the partially invisible and also varied, interwoven instances of power, a growing anomie and uncertainty exists in the various areas of society with respect to social or socially relevant decision (-making) processes and carriers.[214] Examples of this are the currently relevant, defining social expectations concerning education. These stem subordinately from qualified pedagogical experts, let alone from the educatees themselves. The commanders here are primarily transnational political or economic organizations such as the OECD, or the European Union, which are oriented less, or not at all toward pedagogical or educational theory, but rather to economic and/or socio-politically motivated measures (such as those that are justified by anticipated demographic changes, or similar ones).

Furthermore, today, the increasing specialization in the various professional fields is facing the rapidly spreading use of information technologies and thus the significantly improved accessibility of knowledge. This accessibility is connected to a trivialization of formerly exclusive knowledge in all areas of life. The conception of the Enlightenment, which concerned a general knowledge gathered in an encyclopedic form, is deemed outdated in today's information society, respectively in view of an enormous increase in practical knowledge assets on one hand and a diffuse flood of information on the other hand. In educational institutions the focus on general knowledge is largely replaced by a focus on skills, such as competences, priority definitions, or expertise. Formerly fundamental benchmarks, such as truth and sustainability today largely appear as relative (e.g., culturally determined)[215]. The intrinsic value and the fundamental importance of general

---

214 Cf. FOUCAULT [1982] 1988, [1966] 1970 et al.
215 Jacques DERRIDA ([1967] 1978, p. 270 f.) lists here: "[…] *eidos, archè, telos, energeia, ousia* (essence, existence, substance, subject) *aletheia*, transcendentality, consciousness, God, man, and so forth", which ultimately distinguish themselves through differen-

knowledge for the development of personality find limited attention. In this way pedagogy and schools are largely disposed of one of their inherent functions.

It has been found that the admission of uncertainties and a responsible handling of the lack of knowledge in regard to certain action problems, the access to which is limited for explanative knowledge, can become important resources.[216]

It has become clear that human thinking in general and science in particular can reflect reality only in a very fragmented form. Science and the endeavor for enlightenment have not really kept their promises; engaged in power and production conditions, intertwined with military, profit, patriarchal and colonial interests and involved in extremist, e.g. Nazi activities, they can even be considered discredited.[217]

Jean-Francois LYOTARD ([1979] 1984), with his thesis of the so-called "end of the grand narratives", turns against the historically privileged form of rationality. He describes such modern ideas as failed ones that refer to universal and absolute explanation principles (like God, reason, system, class struggle, etc.) and thus force the individual under such a general point of view, levelling all peculiarities. Not least, criticism of science implies a fundamental questioning of deductive approaches. However, even inductive reasoning of scientific findings appears today to be untenable: "In the light of the experimental method, the experience appears to be conservative"[218].

This raises the fundamental question of whether experience, as an essential foundation of science, can ensure the certainty of general knowledge in terms of future-relevant (social) issues (as promised by the noematic concept). It has been shown that complex issues only partially can be broken down analytically, or that a synthesis after an analysis is often incomplete, inadequate or impossible. For the interpretation of one and the same observational data, different, even conflicting theories may be plausible.

In radical approaches, science is, for a variety of reasons, even considered a "transcendental" project.[219] – As an example of the many controversies held in view of the manipulable and science critical circumstances, we will here address that of Karl R. POPPER, who gave the approach of logical empiricism sustained

---

tiation, complexity, shifts, contingencies and breaks. "He locates the difference (différance) in the 'I' itself, since it temporalizes and spatializes. The 'I' is created through a process of 'alteration' and 'deformation'." (Cf. ZIRFAS 2001, transl. by A.K.)
216 Cf. HERZOG 1995; HELSPER et al. 2003; BONSS 2003; BÖHLE et al. 2004; BILSTEIN et al. 2007
217 ADORNO & HORKHEIMER ([1944] 1988)
218 HERZOG & VON FELTEN 2001, p. 23, transl. by A.K.
219 Cf. FEYERABEND 1975

momentum, with the scientific theorist and critic Paul FEYERABEND (1975). The central result of this can be considered the "fallibilism" of POPPER (1992, p. 94): "Science does not rest upon solid bedrock. The bold structure of its theories rises, as it were, above a swamp. It is like a building erected on piles. The piles are driven down from above into the swamp, but not down to any natural or 'given' base; and if we stop driving the piles deeper, it is not because we have reached firm ground. We simply stop, when we are satisfied that the piles are firm enough to carry the structure, at least for the time being." The "scientific method" is thus not a silver bullet to knowledge; it merely secures the "scientific status" of research results, which does not consist in a positive value of the evidence, but only in the verifiability and, primarily, falsifiability of scientific results.[220] In POPPER's view, this status is on one hand the only possible one; on the other hand he considers it to be a potentially deceptive guarantee for the objectivity of knowledge. For POPPER (1979) the scientific acquisition of knowledge is a learning process, during which one will always correct one's own mistakes.

Bearing in mind the preliminary nature of judgments and knowledge profiles, the critique of science is confronted, not at last, with everyday-action, -orientation and -knowledge. In fact, self-restraint is rarely explicitly expressed in science and everyday practice. At the same time, the consciousness of limitation in many areas of everyday practice is (usually implicitly) constitutive for it. For example, only s/he who is aware of the fact that improper action is possible, can, in principle, act appropriately in a situation. Generally, only s/he who expects the lack of understanding of her/his counterpart, or the incomprehensibility of her/his own statements can make her-/himself understood. The acquisition of new knowledge requires an awareness of one's own ignorance, to the extent to which one can oneself get rid of this and which one is prepared for. All forms of knowledge, including knowledge represented linguistic-symbolically, are determined in their acquisition and in their application by the answer they give to the question of how one can get orientation. Such an existential orientation is not specified right from the beginning (if not as common sense, habit, "familiarity trap", or similar etc.). Preliminary decisions are very often only approximate.

In short, for all processes of knowledge acquisition the need to deal with numerous uncertainties plays a central role.

Science also does not differ from the everyday orientation in the way that it constitutes a form of interaction and (often in an unplanned and unreflected way) brings interferences and interventions with it, as shown, for example, in the context

---

220 Cf. POPPER 1969, p. 37

of feminist critique of science[221]. We will come back to this. Scientific judgments can result in a cementing as well as in a change of perceptions concerning their "objects", and, in a broader sense, also of the social conditions.[222] If we understand scientific knowledge as situated, we are not at last confronted with the effects of its application. Pierre BOURDIEU (2002) is therefore committed to ensuring that the questions, perspectives and experiences of those that until now emerged merely as scientific "objects", and not as scientific "subjects", are given space in the scientific area (e.g. in the sense of an empowerment).[223]

For all the similarities, large differences exist in relation to the practice of research and professional activity in educational contexts as well as in terms of the everyday life orientation (such as learning processes), when dealing with imponderables.

Empathy and relationship in the sense of fairness, respectful and giving social contact and collegiality provide the basis for professional action in the teaching profession. These skills do not stand for themselves, they are rather embedded in such social conditions focusing on the individual and joint responsibility for instructional learning processes that take place in teaching.[224] Not only the reflexive-rational analysis of curricular, didactical and pedagogical questions, but also an implicit "know-how" or "finding" ingenousness (see above) is required as a qualification for the acceptance of this responsibility.[225]

The ability of "accurate" judgment and action can, however, not be cast into standards for the professional activity of teachers. The decisions on the "rightness" or "wrongness" of something, as well as on "knowledge" or "lack of knowledge", on "understanding" or "lack of understanding" frequently appear in combination and as a "tertium datur" in everyday practice and in the educational action. The social developments described above can even be read in the sense of anthropological facts as a confirmation of the "tertium datur". This contradicts fundamentally all popular binary concepts of an *either – or,* which are in particular, as pointed out above, the basis for the rational understanding of the world, which science is committed to.

Therefore, one can hold the view that the assumptions of noematic approaches, which have been subsumed, for example, in governmental and metricating

---

221 BUTLER 1990; HARAWAY 1988, 1991, 1997, 2000, or APTHEKER 1989 et al.
222 Cf. BOURDIEU 2002
223 Also HARAWAY 1991, 1997, 2000; APTHEKER 1989; HARDING 1991 et al. – The research approach of Children's Research can be seen as an example of this scientific concern.
224 Cf. RHEIN 2010, p. 45
225 Cf. BERGSTEDT et al. 2012

concepts for teacher education, are generally not reflected critical enough. Some of the problematic points have already been mentioned above.

In the following, more fundamental reasons will be given concerning why purely noematically applied research is considered problematic in the context of instructional and pedagogical questions and challenges:

- There are implicit notions of school education, higher education and education training in the quantitative-empirical educational research on learning and school effectiveness that are not sufficiently reflected. They are not realistically and critically analyzed; this is also true with respect to their formative-and manipulative effects.[226]
- "Objectivity" presupposes, in principle, that the research subjects are by definition clearly distinguishable from one another.
- However, this is not true for an educational relationship, as an educational relationship is always created with the aim of a role reversal. The orientations and knowledge of one (adult) group of agents should not only be made understandable, but gradually also available to the others (the educees). Diverse social processes, such as mimesis and other forms of adoption and adaptation, also transformation, delimitation, directed protest and various forms of social integration and disintegration play a central role here. In the pedagogical fields antinomies often appear that are educatively handled as a "tertium datur". The characteristic signature of educational processes is situational and individual; thus, hardly any objective, universally valid statements can be made about an educational relationship.
- According to the noematic approach, methodical rigour only refers to rational-symbolic reflexivity. Accordingly, Fritz OSER (1997a) places the concept of "reality as text"[227] as the basis of quality criteria of quantitative empirical Social Research (i.e., objectivity, reliability and validity). A "reality as text" in the strong sense is determined by completeness, coherence, clarity and linearity.[228] Scientific results are thus considered to be scientific, if they meet these criteria. The teaching practice is then regarded as a kind of text. That is to say, lessons would consist of engaging in a clearly definable status quo as well as in the practice and the testing of clearly identifiable and retrievable (such as psychometrically identifiable) skills and abilities as well as competences oriented toward specific developmental goals.

---

226 Cf. e.g. MEYER 2009
227 OSER 1997a, p. 215
228 Cf. WULF & ZIRFAS 2007, p. 8

- The fact that the educational reality can at all be viewed as such a "text" is simply presupposed.
- The basic idea of pedagogy, however, is that abilities and skills have to be developed further *within* an educational relationship, before anything else. That is to say, a certain (logical) rigour can only be achieved in an educational context, if it is introduced and even created by the agents in the field.
- Practical pedagogy is dependent on a successful pedagogical *relationship*. The noematic concept of science, however, is based on the possibility of an analytic *control* of the respective subject (or object). The latter is for instance the case if a summative evaluation is used as a final evaluation and review of the performance level of an educational institution, its employees or the pupils. Monitoring and control, however, are forms of one-sided and subliminal, or even open authoritarian interpersonal relationships that are considered not pedagogical, or at the problematic borderline of pedagogy.
- Individual variations, dimly existing and hardly comprehensible things such as emotional states, which are often action-guiding in educational contexts and which characterize learning in item-oriented noematic studies are usually interpreted as confounding factors or error quotients.
- The notion that social agents are not always fully aware of their own perspectively foreshortened perceptions, but that these can be reconstructed scientifically in an objectively comprehensible manner, is bizarre. However, perceptions articulated by the agents in the educational fields can certainly be researched with respect to the accents set here, perspectively foreshortened perceptions, etc.
- Although social relationships can be quite conventionally or habitually structured and defined, they are never universal. In the educational field uniqueness and universality face each other in different ways. The interpretation of the results of noematically designed studies as empirically sound knowledge or as evident facts contradicts in particular the fact that in social contexts nothing but *references* to (possibly only supposedly) universalities are observed, but not these universalities in themselves.
- The valid scientific studies are simply confronted with the everyday, practically oriented, subjective and contextual professional experience of the teacher. From a purely logical standpoint, the two fields of work would thus be incompatible.
- School education is interpreted technologically by the idea that it can be controlled toward success by external input. A straightforward and at any time reproducible application of educational and Human Science theories to practical problems concerning the professional actions of the teachers and a techno-

- logical shortening of the school curriculum prohibit themselves, because the principles of pedagogy and education are eroded if purely instrumental and functionally interpreted.
- With the assumption that the ethos of the teaching profession is in constant development for the sake of lifelong learning, it cannot possibly have output character, or be considered either "good" or "insufficient". Lifelong learning is a willingness and not a measurable result.
- The dignity of educational school practice and its reflexivity can fundamentally be considered not to be determined by scientific facts, or other non-educational orders with a validity claim above the individual level. On the contrary, the ethical duty is to protect this dignity from sociotechnical over-molding. Otherwise there is a risk that pedagogy and with it teaching loses the opportunity and the chance to unfold significant self-reflexive potentials.
- Against the standardization and listing of assessment criteria for "excellent teaching", for a "good school" and, not least, for an "excellent teacher", it is also objected that the Human Sciences as the relevant orientational sciences for practical education have their primary task in investigating what is *considered* good and right and what false and incorrect, and how such ideas are formed.[229] The same is true for practical as well as for theoretical pedagogy. To regard such denominations as given a priori relieves the Human Sciences, and with it pedagogy, of their central task.
- Current theories about a quality development of teaching and learning usually argue from the point of lesson planning. However, this is often related to an undervaluation of the process of the character of education. Brian HUDSON (2008), for example, with his proposal to interpret the teaching research as a "design science" follows a general trend in the Curriculum Studies, the equivalent of Educational Studies and General Education in the English-speaking world. The general object of the "design science" is to do research on the questions, how organization, practices and knowledge influence the "teaching style" of a teacher. The situational and reflexively not easily retrievable dimensions of teaching are hardly taken into account here.
- In the context of metric approaches the fact that education is centrally determined by various knowledge formats and associated with processes of transformation and action uncertainties is usually not considered. Applied to teaching "standards" as well as to collected output of performance-oriented diagnostics, quality assurance and control do not provide information on targeted teaching ways, even if they allege this.

---

229 Cf. BOHNSACK 2007

Control theory models teacher education and the objectifying operationalization of the ethos of the teaching profession obviously miss some important aspects of the relationship between the reflexivity that determines school practice and Educational Science. Therefore, a modeling of teaching and learning processes in general and that of teacher education specifically, which is oriented strictly toward standards, prohibit themselves. An important reason for the fact that the problems that are associated with an application of theory to practical educational challenges are not considered in the noematic perspective is apparently that cognition is understood here exclusively as linguistically-symbolically represented and methodologically sound knowledge. Such knowledge may, for example, play a role related to the resources of schools, or to demographic data. However, such information as well as the knowledge of socio-cultural and -economic developments in certain neighborhoods and/or in the area of school appears helpful and necessary rather for educational and structural, or school organizational decisions than for educational practice.

However, even if the interlocked scientific approaches and the practical knowledge of teachers, which are examined in this essay, are carried only insignificantly by the control standards, the conclusion that it is inadequate to prepare teacher trainees in a science- as well as practice-oriented way does not follow from this.[230]

This challenge can be tackled using the noetic approach. However, the long deep-rooted tradition of the rational paradigm and its philosophically initiated establishment, not least due to policies based on the idea of enlightenment, historically led to the fact that the noematic science is hardly questioned. The noetic paradigm, which operates with many different forms of knowledge and knowledge formats, is not sufficiently introduced and not so common as the noematic one.

2.3 On the Phenomenological Noetic Concept of Science

The predecessors of the noetic research approach are various philosophical and science-critical approaches, which deny the rational science paradigm its absolute claim to validity.[231]

For example, Ulrich OEVERMANN (2001) is critical toward the double structure of rational interpretation patterns: in rational interpretation patterns everyday practice is interpreted on the basis of key concepts as internally consistent. Problems that appear as logical inconsistencies, imponderables, contingencies are

---

230 DEWE 1997, p. 221 ff.
231 A survey of science-critical positions in the 20th Century from the perspective of Cultural Studies is provided by ROUSE (1999), see also LEGGEWIE et al. 2011.

simply perceived as different in principle from these key concepts. In the consequence, the rational patterns of interpretation "[…] seal effectively against arguments that reveal their own inconsistencies"[232]. In this sense the rational research paradigm also suggests to add the flagships of a *general* validity and *objectivity* to judgments which are one-sided, tendentious and led by *partial* perspectives.

A noetic scientific approach wants to avoid and reveal such extrapolations by addressing the far-reaching significance of the imponderable, unplannable and thus, not fully quantifiable and metrizable components of human reality, further by elaborating ways and means of their theoretical, methodological and methodical consideration. The theory-practice relationship is then spelled out quite differently from the current standard noematic science model. The place of hypotheses and the focus on results is replaced by the orientation to perspective knowledge, as for example the dependence of hypotheses and results on various forms and formats of knowledge and thus on a "pluralistic" epistemology.[233]

Here, the noetic science-theoretical conception of course refers to science and not at first to everyday actions, or to actions in the various professional fields.

Even if we are accustomed to regarding our everyday experiences as determined by a variety of contingencies, the indication that research settings and their results also include contingencies is not quite as catchy. It is self-evident that previously secured and approved knowledge can be put in question by new scientific evidence, or perspectives which had not been taken into account.[234] A seemingly valid result can be undermined by external, discursive or other developments such as substantive or cultural contingencies. Some research results turn out to be self-contradictory. However, not only the results but also the research processes are determined by contingencies. In this way unpredictably occurring changes such as unexpected social or natural events can influence a survey, or an evaluation situation. The objects of a setting, or its methods are maybe not completely adequately designed. Perhaps certain impact factors are not considered therein, or similar circumstances. Hidden norms and values may effect a research process and nullify its scientific claim partially, or even entirely. Unresolved, or ignored methodological, methodical and procedural issues may have an effect on a scientific procedure. Doubts may arise concerning the accuracy of knowledge formerly considered as secured due to errors in the process logic, or by such during the choice of the research settings. Sometimes hypostatizations, or other content or

---

232 OEVERMANN 2001, p. 67, transl. by A.K. – However, he draws different conclusions from his thoughts than the noetic research paradigm provides it.
233 Cf. BACHELARD 1971, see above.
234 Cf. RHEINBERGER 2006

methodological inaccuracies are included in the research process. Such deficiencies *undermine* scientific research and its results. Often they are not obvious and require a critical external view to be recognized and reflected.

Nevertheless, there is a research-ethical duty not to ignore, or even cover up these deficiencies. In the noetic perspective, as mentioned, unmindfulness is an integral moment and even the central subject of noetic research. It is assumed that external factors which are not included in the calculations and thus unpredictable as well as those that are owed to a research approach itself require thematic, methodological, methodical and/or practical research implications.

Unlike the noematic concept the noetic conception of science thus does not assume an indubitability of data, not at last sense data, and further does not intend to rely on *pure* thoughts or concepts, either.[235] Under the premise that truth is not simply found and that (– in particular, the social) reality cannot be simply captured empirically, every situation and every concept is perceived much more as determined by diverse and unfathomable conditions and thus by a lack of knowledge. The science-based knowledge development is regarded as principally incomplete.

According to the philosopher Herbert SCHNÄDELBACH (1983) a "research science"[236] is characterized by the fact that it remains in a continuously tested uncertainty about the validity of its own premises;[237] Gaston BACHELARD (1971) speaks of a self-understanding of science, Thomas S. KUHN (1962) of "scientific paradigms" and Karl MANNHEIM (1936) regards research as a social practice.[238]

A noetic scientific approach is always also committed to the framing of its research and engaged in considering all possible framings different from the given or chosen one. Results and objects of research are then considered as subjects to various potential or actual modifications. The preferred object of a noetic scientific approach is the exploration of the respective scopes of research results and knowledge bases. In particular, the methodological, methodical, formal and content aspects of a scientific study are of interest. Omissions, research-implied assumptions, objectives and preconditions are viewed critically. Ways of auditing research results are identified and different perspectives, a subsequent focusing of a research question and new research questions are raised. Viewed from the noetic

---

235 "Concepts are not waiting for us ready-made, like heavenly bodies. There is no heaven for concepts. They must be invented, fabricated, or rather created and would be nothing without their creator's signature." (DELEUZE & GUATTARI [1991] 1994, p. 5)
236 SCHNÄDELBACH 1983, p. 118 ff.
237 HERZOG 2005, p. 313
238 We can not go into further detail here, even if a fundamental study on these different as well as related approaches would be very helpful in our context.

perspective, criticism, the development of perspective, such as cultural formations of a statement and not at last the determination of the consequences of scientifically generated knowledge in social, individual psychological, or other ways, are the prevalent subject of scientific work. It is contemplated whether different ways of thinking and different social relations, cultural traditions and disciplinary contexts, social environments, natural contingencies, research approaches and instruments and technological possibilities result in different academic interests and knowledge formats. A noetic approach understands itself as self-reflexive, respectively it is always concerned with meta-theoretical, such as ethical and methodological issues. As already mentioned, in its reconstruction of knowledge stocks also the alternatives which are conceivable for a particular interpretation of reality, or a certain research process are taken into account.

In short, the focus is on the generation, reasoning and application of knowledge rather than on its simple existence. A noetic approach is concerned not only with scientific design processes, but also interested in the (scientific) logics and contexts of (scientific) practice, i.e. in everyday practical processes, in their geneses and interpretations.

However, knowledge considered as secured is not at all disavowed. It is undeniable that definite knowledge stocks and rationales are employed in scientific contexts as well as in everyday life. Not at last, it structures our living environment. Everyday and professional practices, here also scientific approaches and methods are ascribed to a shared orientation and practical knowledge that is (only) valid in a set context. The determination of such a framework is the subject of noetically inclined research. An evidence of knowledge is not in any case given simply by noetic conception, nor is it ever secured once and for all. Explicit and cognitively available knowledge is, moreover, considered as concomitant and intermingled with factors that are implicit, subluminal, or hidden, and the noetic approach is especially dedicated to such "tacit"[239] contexts. For example, any decision-making or developmental dynamics is questioned, including a research on the treatment of ignorance, misconceptions and uncertainties.[240]

Sometimes also such settings will be created that make it possible to put theoretical assumptions to the test and to reflect on practices in an "oblique" way.[241] Since noetic approaches are not aimed at general results, they only attribute a relative validity to quality criteria of science deemed universally valid by noematic

---

239 Cf. BERGSTEDT et al. 2012
240 Cf. BÖHLE et al. 2004; BILSTEIN et al. 2007; HELSPER et al. 2003; HERZOG 1995
241 Cf. also BECK 1983

definition, such as objectivity, reliability, validity and representativeness, as well as consensus.

2.3.1 Knowledge Forms and Knowledge Formats

Under the perspective that a phenomenon as such cannot be researched, the task of scientific research is seen in particular as defining knowledge forms and formats applied to an object.

Dominant in the field of education is the view of Erich WENIGER ([1929] 1975), who assumes that reality constructions and forms of knowledge are precisely identifiable and distinguishable from each other.

Bernhard WALDENFELS (1990), however, shows that beside cognitively controlled knowledge formats there are also non-conscious, non-intentional, instinctive and automated forms of knowledge, he speaks of "types of rationality"[242]. WALDENFELS' extended rationality term includes all consistent and coherent contexts; – he writes: "I understand rationality in the broadest sense as the essence of meaningful and regular, comprehensive relationships that spread over the different fields of rationality and rationality styles."[243] Different "types of rationality" are not analytically precisely distinguishable from each other. Rather, they mix and influence, disable or encourage each other. They go together in liaisons, eliminate,

---

242 Ludwig FLECK (1980, p. 130, transl. by A.K.) speaks of "styles of thinking" as a "[…] directed perception, with corresponding mental and objective processing of the perceived". According to FLECK something is "true" only within a particular cultural context, in a "collectively shared concept" and tradition of thought. The logic of scientific research can not be reconstructed rationally and formally. The style of thinking determines what is considered true within the collective as a scientific problem, as an evident judgment or as a reasonable method. The thinking style thus determines what is considered a problem within a group up to society, what is an appropriate reaction (method) and how a solution or result of treatment is assessed. Even truth is determined in this way. What is considered as truth can be determined only in the most contemporary style-related resolution of problems: "Such style-related resolution, only singularly possible, means truth. It is not 'relative' or even 'subjective' in the popular sense of the word. It is always or almost always, completely determined by a style of thinking. You can never say the same idea is true for A and false for B. If A and B belong to the same thought collectives, then the idea is either true or false for both. But if they belong to different thought collectives, it is just not the same thought, because it must be unclear for one of them or understood differently by him." (FLECK 1980, p. 131, transl. by A.K.)
243 WALDENFELS 1990, p. 192, transl. by A.K.

or modify each other. Types of rationality do not only determine socially framed practices. They are also evident in cultural phenomena and they are generated, e.g. in scientific studies.

Knowledge forms or formats can thus be established knowledge resources as well as (auxiliary) constructions and methods, implicit or explicit context data. One and the same object is taken in different knowledge formats for different concepts and fields of application (and not least in the relevant sciences). Knowledge stands in a conceptual, technical, situational context, but it can also develop by itself, like when a certain state of affairs is seen in a new context.

It is assumed that the context, the research topic and the raised knowledge formats determine which phenomena, objects and results can be at all expected. This applies quite generally in terms of our knowledge of the world. In the scientific generation of new knowledge as well as in reviewing established knowledge, what is researched and the way how research is conducted and pre-structured by the respective issues and the applied methodologies and methods. In short, facts, phenomena and objects are each known in a very specific way. Our orientative and practical knowledge depends on our knowledge formats.

The object of (noetic) research is to work these knowledge formats out. Wolfgang BONSS, Rainer HOHLFELD & Regine KOLLEK (1993)'s so-called "contextual model of scientific development" within sociological theory model scientific facts, theories and texts are analyzed dependending on the social, practical and theoretical contexts in which they become applicable.

Forms of knowledge and types of rationality or formats of knowledge come into effect, when they are in any way – verbally, materially – referenced. Something will be a stronger attestation for a specific format of knowledge depending on the extent to which, or the way how this knowledge has been generated, is evident or possible (e.g. a vehicle that is screwed together; a manuscript that is revised, a bird's nest which is warp-knitted).

The reconstruction of (generated) knowledge stocks, after this contextualist understanding, takes place with the aim of producing reflexive knowledge. Both are determined, the identified conditions of certain phenomena as well as the knowledge formats employed in their reconstruction.

Knowledge formats are composed of various types of knowledge: generally, explicit and implicit forms of knowledge are distinguished:[244] such forms of knowledge are considered as *explicit* which a subject has strategical control of and which can be expressed linguistically. Explicit *declarative* knowledge, for example, refers to facts and can be written in the form of declarative sentences. Explicit

---

244 Cf. VOGEL 1998, from which the remarks have been taken.

semantic knowledge is abstract world knowledge. Explicit *episodic* knowledge is articulable memory of an experienced situation. With explicit *awareness* knowledge (knowing why) one understands knowledge about why something is as it is (even if sometimes only apparently).[245]

"Tacit"[246] knowledge, however, is not available in the way of strategy, control and expression; Jürgen FUNKE-WIENEKE (2004) determines it closer as a kind of knowledge that is grounded in bodily movements. It comprises the meaning of the *sensory* knowledge transported by the senses as well as the *procedural* knowledge of body practices, further the *knowledge of dynamics*, for example developments, concerning the inherent dynamics of phenomena. This includes the *instrumental* knowledge (knowing how), and the *conditional* knowledge of the situational dependence of actions (knowing when). Implicitly, we also have a *symbolic pre-reflexive* knowledge of the contextual meanings of practices, issues and expectations.[247]

Various forms of knowledge come together in orientation, source, process, or structural knowledge, related to specific circumstances or expectations, or appearing as action, interaction, identity, value, product, expert and managerial knowledge, or as an organizational or milieu knowledge.

An important task of research in the field of noetic research on education, school and teacher education is to determine the relevant knowledge formats for the teaching profession. From the noetic perspective it is particularly important to inspect the handling of the constitutive imponderables for this professional practice.[248]

2.3.2 "Epistemology"

Epistemology is a fundamental branch of philosophy that deals with the question of where knowledge – also in science – originates, what is meant by knowledge and how (or which kind of) knowledge claims legitimacy. Epistemology can be interpreted also as a research approach.[249]

---

245 BONSS 2003, p. 22
246 Cf. BERGSTEDT et al. 2012
247 Cf. HACKL 2006 and the publications by Käte MEYER-DRAWE (2000, 2007, 2008).
248 Cf. BÖHLE et al. (2004) and HERZOG 2005, p. 314.
249 Cf. the analysis of the normativity of approaches that are based on Cognitive Psychology by Helen E. LONGINO (2001). She focuses on the social constitution of knowledge on a pluralistic, simultaneously contextualized, non-relativist basis. The socialized understanding of knowledge production LONGINO conducts in the philosophical practice itself, by transparently presenting her own reflection path throughout the entire

Specifically, according to Gaston BACHELARD (1971), epistemology is understood as empirical/historical mediation of the theory of knowledge and the normative effectiveness of an idea, a theory, or a scientific approach. The philosopher confronts the neo-positivism of his time with the, what he calls "regional" rationality of every science, and he speaks of an "epistemological pluralism". With this he mainly wants to do justice to the fact that scientific concepts do not only differ in their concepts, methods and methodologies, but also in view of the very wide range of possibilities of their practical application.[250]

No general and permanent rules could be set for the extraction of knowledge. He sees the task of science moreover in the analysis of what has hindered the pursuit of scientific knowledge in the past.

In this sense, BACHELARD's approach can be brought into connection with qualitative empirical research, which aims at also (critically) reflecting the viewpoint of the researcher and the respective research context. While quantitative theories in empirical Social Research start with theoretical hypotheses and items that are empirically, often experimentally tested in practice, contexts based on scientific methods, methodically based forms and aspects of the construction of social reality in educational fields are usually reconstructed by using qualitative approaches. In qualitative empirical research practice, theories are generated, or existing theories are extended. Furthermore, in dealing with empirical data, qualitative research has, as spelled out in the sense of BACHELARD's "Epistemology" (1971), the aim to question the methodologies and methods used for the collection and interpretation of the existing theories, and to possibly modify them if necessary or to re-arrange them based on collected field data. In this case under certain circumstances even the view of a practitioner in the educational field can be included in science in a structure-building sense.

In short, high-scale studies could contribute to a closer ("pluralistic") epistemological determination of the position of the subject knowledge and the pedagogical issues related to it.

---

analysis, showing alternative and contrary positions and excluding these normatively according to her own concept definitions.
250 Cf. SMITH et al. 1993

3. Science from the Phenomenological Noetic Perspective

The noetic procedure is determined in every respect by the consideration of the imponderable. It is, as we have seen above, to be understood as a "research science" and as compatible with the "contextualist model of scientific development"[251].

Michele LE DOEUFF (1977) responds to the question of the Archimedean point, from which the sciences generate knowledge, by explaining that this is nothing more than a "space of desire", labeled by an implicit deficit: there is *something* you want to know. – To this we can add, according to Hans-Georg GADAMER ([1960] 1989, p. 363, transl. by A.K.): "In order to be able to ask, one must want to know, which involves knowing that one does not know."[252] A certain lack of knowledge leads to a particular question. Questions and desires for knowledge require an awareness of not knowing and they help us to recognize the possibilities of what is questioned. "The real nature of the sudden idea is perhaps less the sudden realization of the solution to a problem than the sudden realization of the question that advances into openness and thus makes an answer possible. Every sudden idea has the structure of a question. But the sudden realization of the question is already a breach into the smooth front of *popular opinion*"[253].

Accordingly, scientific research has its epistemological base in the consciousness of our prejudiced perception, which is bound to knowledge formats.[254] This position does not change in the noetic understanding of the research process; therefore all knowledge resources are summarized under the sign of the hypothetical.

Noetic research is, therefore, in principle not concerned with contexts of meaning, essence determination and principles. Neither *one* way of being, the *one* idea, the *one* interpretation, the *one* intention and not even the predictable, for example, functional effects of something are the prevalent objects and orientation

---

251 See above and BONSS et al. 1993.
252 In German: "Alles Fragen und Wissenwollen setzt ein Wissen des Nichtwissens voraus – und dies so, daß es ein bestimmtes Nichtwissen ist, das zu einer bestimmten Frage führt."
253 GADAMER [1960] 1989, p. 366, transl. by A.K.; in German: "Das eigentliche Wesen des Einfalls ist [...] weniger, daß einem wie auf ein Rätsel die Lösung einfällt, sondern daß einem die Frage einfällt, die ins Offene vorstößt und dadurch die Antwort möglich macht. Jeder Einfall hat die Struktur der Frage. Der Einfall der Frage ist aber bereits der Einbruch in die geebnete Breite der verbreiteten Meinung."
254 DIEMER 1964

marks of an empirically-based theory generation, as it is usually the case for scientific concepts. The ultimate validity of something, the (one) *proper* justification, or explanation of a situation, or a normative setting, by which an ethical question is treated *correctly*, are also not the scales for scientificity. Universal truths, an available canon of knowledge, such as expert knowledge, or common sense, or the like, are rather the subject of research and they are presented in noetic research results. Reality (not at least social reality) is not determined as a rational structure, that is, as calculable or ultimately determinable. Mental calculation, judgments and rational decisions based solely on binary logic, instrumental thinking and rationality, as well as on routine, systematics and other, clearly signifiable items, or kinds of behavior are, moreover, condemned to fail to reach their aim of making a phenomenon understandable in a general manner. Here, antinomies, abductions, the "tertium datur", "tacit" knowledge (see above), are the prevalent research objects and paths.

A noetic knowledge process wants to "venture out into the open". It is based primarily on knowable (and "finding", see above) orientative and practical knowledge, in which (preliminary) hypotheses and results are linked to explorations in a manner which, in a certain, namely, pre-conscious sense, exhibits stringency. This stringency is considered as antecedent to scientific intentions. Therefore, from the noetic perspective, the adequate knowledge format for the research of a certain matter is carefully selected (from other possible knowledge formats). The selected focus then brings specific methods, questions and a setting with it. Noetic research is generally open for different approaches, or types of knowledge. It is thus always regarded critically whether a selected approach is in fact suitable, or whether a different type of knowledge format should be selected for investigation instead. The ongoing testing whether one's own interpretation and knowledge formats are adequate for the matter is led by one's "finding" orientative and practical knowledge. The continuous assessment of the *correctness* (or *incorrectness*) of an approach or a statement always refers to the *consistent* (or *inconsistent*) conformity of the selected knowledge form and knowledge format with its object.

Basically, various scientific approaches can be described as noetic, in the Social Sciences these are for example (social) constructivist, reconstructive, praxeological, discourse-analytic, system-theoretical, or socio-environmentally motivated research approaches.[255] In the following, the phenomenological, the performativity-theoretical and the praxeological research approach are developed as examples

---

255 "Tacit" dimensions of teaching, such as the implicit knowledge types and formats that occur here, are praxeologically seen as determined by complex action events and procedures. Seen phenomenologically, these are biological aspects of human orientation,

of a noetically understood Social Research. From the spectrum of the different interpretations of these research approaches those will be selected which provide the basis for the further reflections on a science-oriented teacher education.

3.1 On Phenomenological Epistemology

As already pointed out above, according to the phenomenological concept only thetic acts, the "noeses"[256], are given apodictically. The "noema" (see above) is the (following) result of such sense-giving, thetic acts.

Franz BRENTANO (1982) interpreted the phenomenological approach, two centuries ago, as a descriptive *sense imparting* empirical method. This coined its understanding, as it is common today. Since then, various revisions of the phenomenological method have taken place.

For phenomenological approaches the central question is what makes a thing the way *it appears to us*. Thus, the constitutive conditions, respectively the "phenomenality" are of interest in terms of the *how* of an appearance. In the various phenomenological approaches a mutual constitution of self and world is considered in relation to phenomenality: on one hand the phenomenality of an object is determined by the perspectives on it. On the other hand an object has a reference character, meaning it advocates only certain perspectives. From the viewpoint of the mutual constitution of the self, the others and the world, the properties and importance of a phenomenon is elicited in its field(s) of reference.

It is not the place here to expand the various phenomenological approaches in detail. Eidetic or constitution-phenomenological as well body-phenomenological approaches accentuate that the constitution and even the meaningfulness of an object are determined by different perspective, especially through perceptual acts. They emphasize that a phenomenon is to be understood not as directly graspable through description, but as something that appears (differently) according to particular orders and functionalities.

In the following, the body-phenomenological approach is described especially with reference to such approaches coined by Bernhard WALDENFELS and Käte MEYER-DRAWE.

---

considered reconstructively, the tacit dimensions of teaching involve interpersonally shared orientation marks, seen discourse-analytically, these are events of power.
256 See above; HUSSERL [1913] 1983.

3.1.1 Body-Phenomenology and the Concept of a "Constitutive Corporality"[257]

Body phenomenology starts out with the hypothesis of pre-theoretical acts of a constitution of phenomena that are thought of as physical. Logical contradictions are often observed in a pre-theoretical act of insight. Hence, "tertium datur" (see above) and abduction (see above) play an important role in body-phenomenological epistemology. These (uncustomary) modes of consistency can be found within the body-phenomenological theory and are best explicated by the concept of a so-called "constitutive corporeality".

Our living body is essential to us, it is inescapable, and it is largely unavailable to us. It is the complex and existential condition for our existence. The many aspects of our physicality represent an almost incalculable spectrum, which can be detected only in individual aspects and determined empirically.[258] As such our physicality eludes us; we cannot think it, and we cannot influence it on a whole.

However, all body discourses claim to make statements of some kind about the non-speakable part of our physicality. Hence, they principally move, and this is not without problems, at the limit of what can be said. For example, biologist, essentialist, culturalist e.g. social definitions and body constructs arrive at a limit of the existence of the living body. This fact is overlooked again and again. Thus, the immediate and authentic non-constructability of living physicality must always be demanded discursively.[259]

Arnold PLESSNER ([1970] 1980) makes a difference between the "living body"[260] and the "physical body"[261]. We own and have a physical body; PLESSNER ([1970] 1980) speaks of eccentricity and means by this that we self-reflectingly place ourselves outside our (physical) center, referring to our physical body as to an object.[262] We care for our physical body, we train it, modify it, and it is even in our power to kill it. The same is true under certain conditions with respect to the physical body of someone else. The corporeality, however, ultimately eludes the (rational) attempt to make it a subject of discussion, or of control and planning. In its inescapable integrity the body constitutes a counter-support against the encroachments of others. As our original access to reality it is justifiable by nothing

---

257 See also e.g. KRAUS 2010.
258 An initiative in this direction was taken by the author herself, see: http://www.athena-verlag.de/controller.php?cmd=schnellsuche&verlag=1&q=anja+kraus
259 ASMUTH 2006
260 In German: Leib
261 In German: Körper
262 PLESSNER [1970] 1980, p. 368 ff.

else. WALDENFELS (2004a) writes: "The bodily-self is involved in everything, but in a specific way as *someone to whom* [accentuation by B.W.] something happens, [...] *to which* [accentuation by B.W.] he or she answers with sense formation and regulations. Corporeality means that many things concern *myself*, touch *myself* prior to my initiative."[263] The lived body grounds our spontaneous behavior to ourselves and to others. It is constitutive of our experience by determining *how* we perceive something, *how far* we are concerned, it triggers something in us. Our perceived body movements, our emotions, our feelings, our empathy, our understanding of social events are determined bodily. Our living body consists of a variety of processes and states, whether they are organic, such of self-perception and a perception of others, or sensorial qualities. Our body principally determines our relation to ourselves, to others and to the world. As such it is not instrumentalizable or open to manipulation, and it is presupposed to all constructs. Maurice MERLEAU-PONTY proposes a "philosophy as interrogation" that "[...] can consist only in showing how the world is articulated starting from a zero of Being which is not nothingness, that is, in installing, itself on the edge of Being, neither in the for itself, nor in the in itself, at the joints, where the multiple entries of the world cross."[264]

Our orientation lies in the fact that we are in a sense – both subjectively and objectively – *played* on by what is given. The impression to which we are exposed, because we are given to ourselves lively as the body, cannot be planned and calculated in the manner that our corporality or concreteness suggests to us. According to the body-phenomenological concept, this involves resonance and responsive events, meaning we respond physically to something before we become conscious of it. When the body takes a ("responsive") stand to what it is presented in a way by itself, then it modifies by itself to the effects without assimilating. – The phantom arm of an amputee, the inner freedom of a prisoner, our bodies emotions are all phenomena of corporeality, which clarify that the mere physicality of our body is surpassed by its inescapable corporeality. We are also aware of our corporeality, when we do not feel it ourselves in the desired way. When we are sick, feel pain and/or perceive ourselves insensible to certain bodily movements, it becomes clear to us that "[...] the sphere of corporeality is not a homogeneous sphere, which can

---

263 WALDENFELS 2004a, p. 177, transl. by A.K., in German: "Das leibliche Selbst ist an allem beteiligt, aber auf spezifische Weise als *jemand, dem* [Hervorh. durch B.W.] etwas zustößt, zufällt oder widerfährt, *auf das* [Hervorh. durch B.W.] er oder sie mit Sinnbildungen und Regelungen antwortet. Leiblichkeit bedeutet, dass mich vieles an-geht, an-rührt, indem es meiner Initiative zuvorkommt."
264 MERLEAU-PONTY [1964] 1968, p. 260

be augmented or reduced at will. There are more or less central or peripheral parts of the body and body processes, which are characterized by an alternating proximity and distance to the physical self and which affect us with varying intensity. I am more or less, and never myself."[265]

An emphasis is placed on the perception of perspective achievements in terms of object aspects, sensations, knowledge formats, habits, emotions, individual preferences, subliminal thoughts and other orientative values, which enter into a relationship with each other and constitute our world. Inner and extrinsic, empathy and mechanical reactions would be experienced and delivered physically, without being graspable in every respect. The inner awareness of one's own performance and of the performance of the other is contoured physically. Processes of approaching and also those of (self-) alienation, such of shaping and such of deformation are consummated pre-verbally, respectively bodily. Our bodies let us experience the foreign within the familiar. According to Marcel MAUSS (1974) our own body comes into effect as the very first technical means,[266] and the (self-) control and (self-) steering (of the body) are created physically. – WALDENFELS (2004a) writes: The living body acts "[…] as the primeval medium, especially as model and primeval script, but […] also as a primordial resounding plane and original sounding space."[267] In the *how* of our actual experience our past experiences are *written further*, as well as it causes breaks of the continuity of experience.

Our corporeality is evident in the *how* of our perception and interaction with others as well as in the *how* of our actions. Our bodily conveyed experience, our action and orientation knowledge founds our orientation and our practices structuring and instructing these. A schematizing, designing, structuring and interpreting component which is largely spontaneous, implicit, undersigned and somehow taking place en passant is inherent to perception.

Metaphorically speaking, physicality is a kind of an intuitive railing and the primary instrument of control, steering and regulation. At the same time it is an emotional, acoustic receptive soundboard, set to vibrate by other motions, by which meaning is given to us. In the medium of the corporeality, our actions are not at last linked to and determined by our thinking and the knowledge formats. The reference character of corporeality in the sense of experience profiles, activities, physical orders, resonances and orientations conveys to us those constitutions

---

265 WALDENFELS 2004a, p. 203, transl. by A.K.
266 MAUSS 1974, p. 206
267 WALDENFELS 2004a, p. 197, transl. by A.K.; in German: Der Leib wirkt "[…] als Urmedium, speziell als Urbild und Urskript, aber […] auch als ursprüngliche Klangfläche und als ursprünglicher Klangraum."

which substantiate a theory generation. Not only an application of knowledge, but also a pre-rational concept formation takes place in the body. The reference character of the corporeal self is evident, for example, if we are internally aware of our own and external (inter-) actions, or if we orient ourselves on unfamiliar terrain.

In short, the body-phenmenological method looks at phenomenality in the sense of bodily conveyed constitution processes, or "noeses".[268] It focuses the underlying structures of meaning of a (an everyday or scientific) theory of "diverse realities"[269], as well as the regulatory functions and the control systems, according to which they come to light.

3.1.2 On Body-Phenomenological Epistemology

WALDENFELS (1992) writes: "The object is not simply one and the same, it proves to be the same in the exchange of ways of awareness and intention in which it glimpses from close or from a distance, from this or that side, in which it is perceived, remembered, expected or fantasized, in which it is evaluated, treated or sought, in which it is claimed as real, is put down as possible or doubtful, or is negated."[270] Perceiving is perceiving *as*, heard makes sense *as* heard, thought *as* thought. Thetic acts (noeses) constitute the phenomenality. Due to a presentation that is often imperceptible, diverse and heterogeneous a phenomenon is accessible

---

[268] WALDENFELS 1994, p. 29
[269] SCHÜTZ 1945
[270] WALDENFELS 1992, p. 15, transl. by A.K.; in German: "Der Gegenstand ist nicht einfach ein und derselbe, er erweist sich als derselbe im Wechsel von Gegebenheits- und Intentionsweisen, in denen er aus der Nähe oder aus der Ferne, von dieser oder von jener Seite erschaut, in denen er wahrgenommen, erinnert, erwartet oder phantasiert, in denen er beurteilt, behandelt oder erstrebt, in denen er als wirklich behauptet, als möglich oder zweifelhaft hingestellt oder negiert wird." Edmund HUSSERL ([1931] 1982 § 17, transl. by A.K.) writes: "[...] Thus the near-thing, as 'the same', appears now from this 'side', now from that; and the 'visual perspective' change – also, however, the other manners of appearance (tactual, acoustic, and so forth), as we can observe by turning our attention in the right direction. Then, if we pay particular heed to any of the die's features that show itself in the die-perception (for example: the die's shape or color, or one of its faces in particular, or the square shape or particular color of the face), the same is again the case. Always we find the feature in question as a unity belonging to the passing flow of 'multiplicities'. Looking straightforwardly, we have perhaps the one unchanging shape or color; in the reflective attitude, we have its manners of appearance (orientational, perspectival, and so forth), following one another in a continuous sequence."

as a thing to us and in this way it is also available to our thoughts and actions. It will never be evident as such, but as perceived aspects and as perspectives which are presented to it.

The phenomenological research approach is therefore considered a "[…] process of interaction between the researchers and their subject ('something appears as something')."[271] WALDENFELS (1998) refers to phenomenology also as the "doctrine of viewpoints"[272].

The phenomenological sciences aim to cater to these constitutional processes by the most accurate, orderly and unbiased description of the possible approach(es). Here, phenomenological research claims its starting point not in theory, but in the everyday world.[273] In the phenomenological understanding of science the researcher standpoint is not that of a sovereign observer who is capable of a lucid self-reflection and external observation. What is perceived is neither theoretical speculations nor constructions.

In distinction from "hypothesis" and "design" as the popular options to grasp the cognitive activity of a subject scientifically, WALDENFELS (1998) employs the principle of responsiveness methodically: a perception is a specific *answering* to something that *affects us, excites us, calls to us*. The claim to which is replied here is to be understood on one hand in terms of an *appeal*. On the other hand it is a pretension, an *entitlement to something*. S/he who is addressed will participate in the events in the dative by noticing something *herself/himself*; something will happen to *her/him*, and it triggers something in *her/him*, without this being intended by *her/him*. The act is thus not confined to the embodiment of one's own designs or intentions, it begins elsewhere; the answer will testify to the imposed appeal, or claim to which it responds.

The phenomenological method, the so-called "phenomenological reduction" or "epoché" is designed to reflect methodologically and methodically the constitution of phenomena within the meaning of viewpoints. It should in particular do justice to the fact that the phenomenological process of analysis is applied to the aim of reflecting the researcher standpoint in regard to the various sense-making processes that reshape it. An "epoché" is meant as a fundamental change of attitude in which an opinion or interpretation which is presented to the subject

---

271 HILDENBRAND, B. 1991: preface to STRAUSS, p. 12, cited according to WALDENFELS 1998, p. 50, transl. by A.K.
272 WALDENFELS 1998, p. 50, transl. by A.K.
273 This corresponds with the fact that Ernst MACH (1980), one of the founders of qualitative Social Research, determines scientific methods closer as "reflected everyday methods".

is to be inhibited with the aim of becoming aware of the subject as a sensual-acting, as ineffable perceptions, as subliminal thoughts and as the origin of speech in silence.[274] According to MERLEAU-PONTY ([1961] 1993) an object opens up for us through the pre-rational, pre-predicative and pre-reflexive as the unreflexive moments of consciousness. Therefore, the phenomenality of a thing opens up to us as the contouring of "limits" and as the identification of various "exclusions". The constitution of phenomena is detected mentally and thus to a certain extent in an inverse way, namely by contouring the limits and exclusions of thinking in a "phenomenological reduction". Thereby, the constructions which are presented to a subject come into view. Under inclusion of common perceptions, constructions and (pre-) hypotheses the phenomenological method focuses on the modalities of the coming-into-appearance and the genesis of a thing, on responsive processes and recursions (repetitions within the meaning of resuming). Aware that the standpoint assumed in a "phenomenological reduction" in any case only allows a limited viewpoint modeling of an object, the obtained insights will be subjected to an interpretation over and over and in a potentially infinite regress, in a "referral back to phenomenology itself".[275]

WALDENFELS (1998) substantiated the phenomenological knowledge work also with the concept of difference. More precisely, he shows that a detection of the "logos of phenomena" as the *how* of their occurrence in the combination of content and access mode presupposes the observance of diverse varieties of difference. In the "phenomenological reduction" a "different vision", "different hearing", or the like, was to be implemented in the sense of "perspective shifts", view alienations and as modes of "deviation". The targeted object then comes into effect to the extent to which the respectively occupied viewpoint or standpoint develops the specific manner of *how* respectively the form *in which* something presents itself (to us), or "[...] how at a time something in view comes to action or speech"[276].

Käte MEYER-DRAWE (2008) describes the phenomenological method, or reduction as an "oblique observation"[277] that tries to capture the pre-rational, pre-predicative and pre-reflexive as the unfiltered by reflection.[278] The oblique reflection is not a simple perception (or bringing to mind) of internally existing ideas, but it is linked to the particular situation a phenomenon is perceived. To

---

274 MERLEAU-PONTY [1961] 1993
275 WALDENFELS 1998, p. 20
276 WALDENFELS 1998, p. 22, transl. by A.K. While *what*-questions presuppose that they can be answered by a stable characterization or by a definition, *how*-questions are applicable for the description of cultural phenomena.
277 MEYER-DRAWE 2008, p. 2
278 MEYER-DRAWE 2008, p. 118

tap into an object of thought in the manner of *how, or in which form* it presents itself, respectively as the "[…] manner in which something comes into view, action or speech"[279] means to capture that which is athematic to the consciousness. Then comes into effect, as Iso KERN (1975, p. 76 f., transl. by A.K.) points out, an "oblique" repetition of consciousness: while in the direct reflection the envisioned consciousness is simply repeated (e.g. in memory I see again the chamois), "[…] a more complex basic form of realization mirrors the reflection in a more pregnant sense, the repeated consciousness is no longer *concordant*, no longer in the same direction of interest, but a turn-over, or *re-orientation* is taking place by no longer directing an interest towards that to which the envisioned consciousness, or its mere reproduction. The intention is oriented, moreover, bent back on any athematic moment of the same in the envisioned consciousness. It captures any moment in the envisioned consciousness, which indeed belongs to this consciousness, but is not objective in itself"[280].

Spontaneous reactions, intuitions, immediate understanding, empathy, or expressive qualities are therefore ways of realization. While the (physical) phenomenological understanding of science is focused on the fundamental determination of its purpose and the possibility of knowledge, the performativity-theoretical understanding of science is oriented at a theory of action.

3.2 On Performativity-Oriented[281] Epistemology

Like the body-phenomenological theory construction, the performative epistemology has no universalistic claim. Under the performative paradigm the largely dominant thought model of mental representation of (e.g. educational) reality is

---

279 WALDENFELS 1998, p. 22, transl. by A.K.
280 In German: Während in der direkten Reflexion das vergegenwärtigte Bewusstsein sozusagen geradewegs wiederholt werde (z.B. in der Erinnerung sehe ich nochmals die Gemse auf einer Bergkuppe), "[…] spiegelt eine komplexere Grundform der Vergegenwärtigung, die Reflexion im prägnanteren Sinn, das wiederholte Bewusstsein nicht mehr *gleichsinnig*, nicht mehr in gleicher Interessenrichtung, sondern in einer Umwendung oder *Umorientierung*, indem sie ihr Interesse nicht mehr auf das richtet, worauf das vergegenwärtigte Bewusstsein bzw. dessen bloße Reproduktion, thematisch achtet, sondern ihre Intention auf irgendein im vergegenwärtigten Bewußtsein unthematisches Moment desselben zurückbiegt. Sie erfasst irgendein Moment im vergegenwärtigten Bewußtsein, das zwar in dieses Bewußtsein gehört, aber in ihm selbst nicht gegenständlich ist."
281 The analysis by Doris KOLESCH (1999) provides an overview of the history of the concept of performativity since the 1950s.

formance. Explicit and not explicit social and cultural meanings which prime and accompany an action create a so-called "conjunctive" space of experience that is shared by the actors in the field. In other theoretical contexts performativity is considered not only fundamental to the social and cultural action, but also to any orientation activities.

For example DELEUZE ([1968] 1994) places "performativity" in the context of his concept of "repetition" and "difference". This concept is intended as an alternative to the representative model of thought: Any identification (of characters) occurs in a repetition in which a certain character is detached from its singular context and placed in another. DERRIDA ([1967] 1978) establishes "difference" and "repetition" as an opposition structure of language, according to which each character gets its value due to its distinction from another character. Repetition is not interpreted as unity and equality in itself and not as the creation of one-and-the-same. Repetition, moreover, induces a fundamental difference. Such "difference" can not be reduced to contradiction. A matter gets its valence by shifting or repetition, without something that is shifted first, or is the original. These valences or meanings are identified by the differences that occur in the processes of repetition. It is of interest how a thing is, respectively how it is brought into view *differently*. An example which shows that reality is generated in a performative way by repetition is given by the interpersonal understanding: Usually it becomes clear only in the course of a conversation, first, how the utterances of a conversation partner/ interlocutor are, or could be meant, and, second, how oneself thinks about the topic of the conversation.[290] The creation of meaning which is decisive for the understanding, such as the comparison of the current with the previously experienced, the specification of what is implied in a statement, as well as the relationship events and the therein accomplished balance of interests etc., primarily take place implicitly. This means that there are elements of tacit knowledge, effective circumstances, or situational interpretations as an implicit and essential surplus to a visible and describable, possibly expectable effect. WULF & ZIRFAS (2007) describe the performativity-theoretically established scientific understanding accordingly: "A performative understanding as a methodological approach in Social and Human Sciences aims for observable *regularities* [accentuation by C.W. & J.Z.] including the conditions of possibility and of impossibility of social action as repetition and modification."[291] An analysis of performative processes thus takes

---

290 Cf. VON KLEIST [1805/6] 2004
291 WULF & ZIRFAS 2007, p. 9, transl. by A.K.; in German: "Ein performatives Verständnis als methodische Vorgehensweise in den Sozial- und Humanwissenschaften zielt auf beobachtbare *Regelmäßigkeiten* [Hervorh. durch C.W. & J.Z.], die die Bedingungen

place ambiguously: on one hand, it seeks visible events, the structure of which results from "repetition" and "difference". On the other hand, the genesis of this structure will be investigated. So, based on the paradigm of performativity, the way in which and with what result scientific and everyday approaches *make use* of language with the aim of presenting reality as orderly and rationally comprehensible can be figured out. Linguistic statements or other actions, also methods and structures are examined about their interpretations of the world and about the resulting conditions they lead to. As a prime example of the effect of linguistic statements such social situations are given for which the being and meaning is rooted in social recognition, such as the gesture of a greeting that implicitly refers to social roles, status differences, etc.[292]

In short, performativity-theoretically based research is, like the phenomenological one, determined by the effort of self-restraint with regard to the interpretations presented to a cause as well as by the research ethos of the greatest possible transparency of the research intention(s).[293] The, principally, hypothetical nature of the descriptions of reality is established; the aim is to bracket everyday prejudices as well as the prejudiced texture of reality.

Donna J. HARAWAY (1997) developed a scientific approach based on performative processes, which understands itself as a critique of science today. More specifically, she confronts the idea of scientifically valid representation with her "non-essentialist feminist standpoint theory"[294]. Regarding the traditional self-conception of Social and Human Sciences, HARAWAY critisizes that they claim for themselves (within strict disciplinary boundaries) to be able to determine what is real. She accuses these disciplines of assuming an impossible position, namely a reflexive place outside the real, immanent one.

HARAWAY (1988) thus wants to replace the goal of *valid* and *objective* research by a "practice of objectivity", which deals with the question of how objectivity is constructed or created. The aim of the research, as designed by her, is to elicit what claims to be singular and what general application. *Subjectively-singular-speculative* and *objective-universal-evident* in her view do not describe subject matters but rather two different aspects of the figuration of sociality and thus also performative judgment. In a social context an individual-subjective on one hand and

---

der Möglichkeit wie der Unmöglichkeit sozialen Handelns als Wiederholungen und Veränderungen beinhalten."
292 Cf. AUSTIN 1975 and cf. the discourse concept introduced above.
293 With respect to the conceptualisation of the (research) intention very different positions are subsumed under the generic concept of empirical phenomenology, which are however not part of the discussion here.
294 HARAWAY 1997, p. 305

a universality-claiming access on the other hand become evident, for example, when performative reference is made to subjectivity or to universality.

If singularity and universality, or universal validity apply here as moments of performative processes, among others, and not as adequate description modes for (performativity-theoretical) research results, then the generalization of scientific results prohibits itself, and it raises the question what the specific systematics, rigour and usefulness of performativity-theoretical scientific analysis are alternatively based on.

First of all, the importance of performativity for human thought and action is considered to be fundamental; the concept of performativity describes the systematic character of research: "The performativity captures us within the theory creation".[295] (Scientific) observing and writing, comprehending, understanding and interpreting are primarily implementations of action and not thinking; at the same time, specific context-creating conditions are determinative for these. According to HARAWAY (1997), this also applies to the methodologically sound installation and testing of hypotheses, to methodologically-based analyses as well as to the presentation of scientific results. She represents here the concept of a "radical performativity"[296], about which Edvin FORSTER (2007) writes: "Radical performativity recognizes that knowledge and its production are the consequences of hybrid processes. Hybrid is a provisional term introduced to express the fact that with knowledge production certain perspectives to see are coproduced, which, in turn, strike back to the knowledge producers and their productions and thereby create new productions. After all, as advocated by radical performativity, Human Sciences cannot avoid to pursue the *implicit violence in our visualization practices* [accentuation by E.F.] with passionate impartiality – on behalf of a concrete vision."[297] Sciences in general are thus understood as social practices that reproduce the balances of power, and thus as actions that follow certain social rules which they reproduce, sometimes in an altered, incomplete, one-side accentuated, not entirely anticipatable, or otherwise unfinished way. Social Sciences oriented toward a "radical performativity" are primarily concerned with analyzing action-related (social) contexts as what they are, rather than in a general context. The focus of analysis lies on the potentials of a questioning of existing hegemonies and a breaking with them. Therefore, the process structure and context-dependence of phenomena are of primary interest. Attention, or scientific importance is principally directed, and attributed to practices and less to theories or hypotheses,

---

295 Cf. BRAMBERGER 2007, p. 104, transl. by A.K.
296 KRÄMER & STAHLHUT 2001, p. 55 ff.
297 FORSTER 2007, p. 234, transl. by A.K.

and forms of planning, strategy and calculation. Here, the emergent and relative character of knowledge forms and knowledge formats is in view. This means that knowledge forms and formats are not simply regarded as given, but as relative and arising under certain conditions.

Such conditions can be e.g. power-related. Then, a performative interpretation of science involves an analysis of implicit forms of power. – The usual thinking in dichotomies such as subject and object, or master and servant is not considered defining for such an analysis. Further, the definition and decision-making power is not attributed to specific persons. Theories are, moreover, regarded as controlled and discrete series of events.[298] Such "events" can be people or things, but also environments, concepts, systems and strategies, or modes of implementation, practices and their effects, contexts, or the like. Thus, relationship events, situational condition fields and appearing centers of action are of interest.[299] The agents as well as the institutions do not play a central role here. For example, in school education, specific actions (such as playing cards) can be used to create a relational axis between something (e.g. the media world such as Star Wars) and a pupil group, with latent educational effects.

The methodological considerations of HARAWAY (1997) have their origin in the social constructivist approach (in e.g. the interpretation of Michel FOUCAULT and Judith BUTLER), according to which language does not merely represent reality, but also contributes to its constitution and change: each formulation is an intervention in reality.[300] According to BUTLER (1990), the construction of a range of (social) deviations goes hand in hand with normality constructions. BOURDIEU pleads for an "engaged knowledge"[301], and thus for engaged sciences. Bettina APTHEKER (1989) formulates the corresponding socio-political demand: "[…] we have to allow for this ambiguity and paradox, respect each other, our cultures, our integrity, our dignity."[302]

---

298 FOUCAULT [1966] 1970
299 Cf. HARAWAY 2000
300 Cf. FORSTER 2007, p. 230, transl. by A.K.
301 BOURDIEU ([2002] 2009) writes: "[…] in fact, you have to be an independent scholar, who works in accordance with the rules of scholarship to be able to produce an engaged scholarship, that is a 'scholarship with commitment'. To be a truly engaged scholar, you must be legitimately engaged, engaged in knowledge. And this knowledge is not acquired except by the work of scholarship, undertaken according to the rules of the scholarly community."
302 APTHEKER 1989, p. 253

In short, the performativity-theoretical research, so HARAWAY, points out the "design character"[303] of theory creation with the aim to uncover ingrained forms of definition and decision-making power. The scientific approach based on "radical performativity" is dedicated to the even broader programme of a liberation from the (final) *desire* and *obligation to affirm* something as a definite object, for the benefit of the claim, "[...] to understand an event in its context – in a context, which is simultaneously exceeded by this event."[304]

From a methodological perspective, HARAWAY (1988) argues for "situated knowledges" and a fully movable thinking as a permanent critical reflecting on its own contextual references and connections. She is concerned with taking a "partial perspective"[305] and she pleads for an accumulation of knowledge that is "[...] never finished [...] is always constructed and imperfectly stitched together, and *therefore* [stressed by D.H.] able to join with another."[306] She argues thus for "[...] a doctrine and practice of objectivity that privileges contestation, deconstruction, passionate construction, webbed connections, and hope for transformation of systems of knowledges and ways of seeing."[307] This involves subluminal aspects of tasks, establishments and actions.

For the methodological-methodical sensibilisation[308] of implicit knowledge and process forms HARAWAY (1997) suggests the following methodological approach:

Research that takes the necessary performative character of theory into consideration has its starting point in the "passionate detachment"[309] as well as in the

---

303 Jacques DERRIDA describes the design of a theory as a "jetty": "By the word 'jetty' I will refer [...] to the *force* of that *movement,* which is not the *subject, project,* or *object,* not even rejection, but in which takes place a production and any determination, which finds its possibility in the jetty – whether that production or determination be related to the subject, the object or the rejection." (DERRIDA 1989, p. 65; accentuations by J.D.)
304 WULF & ZIRFAS 2007, p. 33, transl. by A.K.; in German: Der sich an "radikaler Performativität" orientierende wissenschaftliche Ansatz verschreibt sich sogar der noch weitergehenden Programmatik einer *Befreiung* vom (endgültigen) *Bestimmen-Wollen* und auch *-Müssen* eines Gegenstands zugunsten des Anspruchs, ein "[...] Ereignis in seinem Kontext zu verstehen – in einem Kontext, der von diesem Ereignis zugleich überschritten wird." (Hervorh. durch C.W. und J.Z.)
305 "Only partial perspective promises objective vision" because it is based on "limited location and situated knowledge, not about transcendence and splitting of subject and object" (HARAWAY 1988, p. 583).
306 HARAWAY 1988, p. 586
307 HARAWAY 1988, p. 191f.
308 Cf. DOHMEN 2001; FRANK, GUTSCHOW & MÜNCHHAUSEN 2005
309 HARAWAY 1988, p. 192

socio-political and emancipatory claim of a "non-mindless commitment to situated knowledges"[310]. The quality criterion imposed on science by Gilles DELEUZE and Félix GUATTARI ([1991] 1994, p. 28) should apply: "If one concept is *better* [accentuation by G.D & F.G.] than an earlier one, it is because it makes us aware of new variations and unknown resonances, it carries out unforeseen cuttings-out, it brings forth an Event that surveys (survole) us." In the context of "operative-strategic"[311] scientific theory creation interventions in a given setting are, under certain conditions, made with the aim of discovering, or developing terms. For example, alternative scenarios, by which existing theories can be questioned, are introduced with the aim of showing the "design character" of social and human-scientific theory creation. – Ralf BOHNSACK (2007) writes: "[…] the cultural and socio-scientific observer [has] to ask: *how* [accentuation by R.B.] that which is believed to be true and correct, or that which is excluded as untrue and false, can be *created* [accentuation by R.B.] in everyday practice and in its socialization history, in its sociogenesis"[312]. BOHNSACK (2007) argues that Social and Human Sciences are, in principle, not entitled to any other than the performative form of knowledge. Because: subject "[…] of a valid social scientific observation are [… and always have been, A.K.] not the motives and subjective intentions themselves, but merely the processes of their construction, that is their interpretive and definitional performativity."[313] However, qualitative research has yet to develop an adequate language for describing the inner regularity and self-dynamics of the interpretation of social phenomena.[314] The definition of such a description language is also the aim of certain praxeological approaches.

---

310 HARAWAY 1997. In the background of her argumentation stands the interest in the consistent scattering of traditional images of femininity and their consequences for human condition today. The "not-senseless commitment to representations" also applies to the rehabilitation of the deposed human body in terms of the prominence of the parallelism of different "designs" (see above).
311 KRÄMER & STAHLHUT 2001, p. 55 ff.
312 BOHNSACK 2007, p. 201, transl. by A.K.
313 BOHNSACK 2007, p. 202, transl. by A.K.
314 BOHNSACK 2007, p. 208

3.3 On Praxeological Epistemology

"Praxeology" is an extremely enigmatic concept.[315] This can be attributed to the fact that, in the field of Philosophy and Sociology, the term generally refers to theories of action (even those that are attributable to the noematic science paradigm).

In particular, the term praxeology refers to a specific researching access which is interested in methods and practices and which is, in turn, separated from other action-theoretical approaches. – BOURDIEU ([1972] 1977, [1980] 1998) for example, defines praxeology as opposed to phenomenology and objectivism.[316]

The latter definition refers primarily to the fact that in the praxeological interpretation of human action BOURDIEU wants to generally exclude the possibility of a stringent recursion to universal and lasting knowledge of the world.[317] The focus is rather on local knowledge forms and formats. These are considered as crucial not only for everyday, but also for professional, e.g. for scientific practices. Georg BREIDENSTEIN (2008) writes: "In praxeological approaches the social one is no longer considered part of normative orientations nor, as assumed in *rational choice* [stressed by G.B.] approaches, of the decisions of the actors, it is common in classical theories of action. Social orientation is rather grounded in everyday social practices themselves, which are determined by practical knowledge and practical skills. A *practice* [stressed by G.B.] is therefore the smallest unit of the social context; it is a routinized 'nexus of doings and sayings'(Schatzki 1996, p. 89), which is held together by an implicit *practical understanding* [stressed by G.B.]. With the accentuation of practices the view is withdrawn from the *actor* [stressed by G.B.]. So it is not about the question of who carries out which practice, but conversely about who, or what is *involved* [stressed by G.B.] in a specific practice. Human bodies, as well as artifacts are considered 'participants' of practices. (Hirschauer 2004) Thus, the praxeological perspective insists on the materiality of events or practices: 'A practice *consists* [stressed by A.R.] of certain routinized movements and activities of the body' (Reckwitz 2003, p. 290)."[318] BREIDENSTEIN (2008) further emphasizes that with the praxeological perspective it is assumed, "[…] that in the social world not individual discrete social *practices* occur in isolation, but rather the social world constitutes *loosely coupled complexes* [stressed by A.R.] of practices (Reckwitz 2003, p. 295)"[319].

---

315 For the relationship between body phenomenology and praxeology see KRAUS 2013.
316 However, he does not consider the diversity of the phenomenological approaches.
317 For this question, phenomenological approaches apply very differently.
318 BREIDENSTEIN 2008, p. 206, transl. by A.K.
319 BREIDENSTEIN 2008, p. 206, transl. by A.K.

Accordingly, Hannah ARENDT ([1958] 1998, p. 183 f.) writes: "The realm of human affairs, strictly speaking, consists of the web of human relationships which exists wherever men live together. The disclosure of the 'who' through speech and the setting of a new beginning through action always fall into an already existing web, where their immediate consequences can be felt. Together they start a new process which eventually emerges as the unique life story of the newcomer, affecting uniquely the life stories of all those with whom s/he comes in contact. It is because of this already existing web of human relationships, with its innumerable, conflicting wills and intentions, that action almost never achieves its purpose; but it is also because of this medium, in which action alone is real, that it 'produces' stories with or without intention as naturally as fabrication produces tangible things." By our acting we thus place a thread in a fabric that is not made by us. Although action is certainly started by individuals, it refers to others. Hereby, the action not only finds its justification and its continuation, but also the modes of action are determined. Action therefore always tuned intersubjectively and bound to a socially mediated position; it has its actual place in a social and material context.

To come back to praxeology, one can say that the modes how (scientific) theories are (can be) applied to the professional practice of teachers become clear by practices. Often, educational practices e.g. interpret common language games, like the slogan *equal opportunities for all,* as their key objectives. A learning support then takes into account individual starting positions for learning. On this basis, the process of initiating learning is practically configured individually, or as an integrated part of the individualized competence development.

Praxeological interpretations of a notion, idea, or of an image can be supplemented with studies of the focal points of *effective* thinking and acting, for example in school practice. Effectiveness, however, is not understood here in the sense of a secured result or output. With *effective* thinking and action in this context we mean that a social interaction event leads to initiating, directing and reflecting learning as well as to educational processes.

It is not assumed that a praxeological interpretation can achieve the same transparency, precision and suitability for theory and empirical research as it is possible or allegedly possible by a purely theoretical, rational and categorical point of view. Thus, in the praxeological perspective especially transfigurations, contradictions or limits of understanding and interpreting are made visible. It can, for example, be made clear that distinct educational ideals and standards in practice are adjoined in many ways by their opposite. Concepts and practices sometimes come into conflict with each other; it can also become clear that concepts can only approximately be congruently put into practice.

In short, in the praxeological perspective breaks, contradictions, or aspects of a mixing of divergent directives and practices usually become evident. It can be assumed that the action-concomitant reflexivity, which was established above as typical of the teaching profession, can be determined in more detail praxeologically.

In view of the contradictions which are recognizable from the praxeological perspective, the above outlined fields of tension become particularly apparent with respect to schools and education. If every educational measure poses the task in many different facets, for example, to dissolve contradictions that occur between specificity and generality to one side or the other, a kind of Janus face results. The antagonism of its viewing directions depending on the situation at hand can be investigated by a praxeologically-oriented practice research.

In the following, the necessary reflexivity for the development of teaching will be explained with respect to the noetic-epistemological background. That is to say, (only) some challenges for a phenomenological, performativity-theoretical or praxeological study on the task area of school teachers will be outlined. Because of the complexity of this research and study area there is no claim for systematization, completeness and deepening; this claim will be raised in another study.

4. The Epistemology of Science-Oriented Teacher Education and Empirical Approaches to Orientative and Practical Knowledge of Teachers

Formative effects of science on school and teaching practice are usually not intended, and they are not considered systematically, also not in ethical terms. If, however, the formative effects would be principally recognized and systematically identified in science, new perspectives and opportunities would open up not only for scientific reflexivity, but also for the science orientation in teacher education.

According to BACHELARD (1971) and the noetic approach, such effects are regarded merely as given. In the so-called "integration concepts"[320], which emanate from a congruence of skills and knowledge in the teaching profession (see above), the relationship between theory and practice in the teaching profession is modeled.

This perspective surpasses the framework set by this essay. Here, the question of a science- and at the same time practice-oriented teacher education is posed, based on the issue of a hiatus between the knowledge forms and formats and the scientific legitimacy of their actions and judgment, as applied in the classroom by the teacher.

It is argued that the everyday practical, the professional and the scientifically-noetic activity – inspite of all existing differences – show similarities when viewed with respect to theories of perception and action. There are parallels between the practical teaching actions and noetic Science Research, especially when it comes to the conditions of success and failure of practices. As for professional actions in the teaching profession, noetic research is confronted with the insight into the limitations of its own designs and, based on these, it generates methodologically-founded reflexive knowledge. In addition, different knowledge formats, such as forms of orientative and practical knowledge, or the meaning shared by actors in the field, come into view and are subject of analysis in both fields.

Until now, scientific research plays a role in academic and curricular decisions mainly when these legitimize a circumstance in a purely argumentative, i.e. symbolic-linguistic way.[321] However, such highlighting of the linguistic-symbolic knowledge mode appears problematic, especially because its praxeological rele-

---

320 Cf. NEUWEG 2010, see above.
321 E.g. developments in the Educational Sciences, Technical Sciences and Research on Didactics are reported; references are suggested sometimes in the curricula or in official regulations.

vance is highly controversial in terms of instructional decisions:[322] Legitimation knowledge and the ability to use solid arguing, as well as a broad conceptual knowledge per se evidently do not guarantee for a successful teaching practice. The opposite may even be the case. When teachers argue in a science-oriented manner,[323] they usually do not legitimate their acting in the context of heteromorphic normativity, which effectively determines their actions, but rather often by discourses that are far from the action and have a more or less theoretical character. The symbolic-abstract knowledge in the educational field then gets attached to a too large practical relevance. Power-related discourses and symbolically disguised "familiarity traps" are then possibly inflated to be professional knowledge.

School pedagogy and teacher education are particularly vulnerable to this. However, in the context of teacher studies at the university, such justifications are *rehearsed* over a wide range today. A theory-practice transfer which has to be achieved during the academic studies should be based on cases and case research as well as on learning settings that make it possible to reflect on professional as well as on scientific practices, e.g. by critically reflecting subjective theories in terms of "familiarity traps".

In this paper, it is argued that the principally non-conclusive competence development of teachers can be modeled less by the (scientifically legitimable) *results* in school and education or by a *code* of professional ethics, but rather as *practices* and *processes* in the educational profession. Here the focus is on the "plurality of the logical forms of practice"[324] of practical school activities. It is assumed that professional practices follow knowledge forms and formats which usually include (individual) profession theories.

If, as BÖHLE et al. (2004) emphasize, the ability to flexibly respond to unplanned and unpredictable is in the focus of (every) professional action, it is not of primary importance in the professional training to relate coherent ethical maxims of one's own actions and judgment to the professional field, but rather to make such maxims reflexively available. This can be done in the first place, as for example VAN MANEN (1995) shows, by a revision of assumptions and prior experience. The ability to communicate already internalized situational interpretations skillfully with new experiences, interpretive schemes and styles of thinking is central for the professionalism of teachers. Such experience formation should be part of teacher education in a scientifically grounded manner. That is to say,

---

322 Cf. NEUWEG 2005
323 BÖHME 2004, p. 134
324 EHRENSPECK & RUSTEMEYER 1996, p. 379, transl. by A.K.; in German: "Pluralität eigenlogischer Praxisformen".

meaning-making through practices, a revision of biases, and experiential learning should be methodologically supported. The methodological and methodical inventory is provided by the noetic scientific approach.

This raises the question of what is visible of the plurality of the logical forms of practice and can thus be established scientifically and empirically and conveyed in the context of teacher education. According to the noetic approach, science can, by means of its analytical angle, pave ways by which classroom situations can be dealt with in a "finding" manner. For example, it can allow the analysis of the normative heterogenous framework of an educational situation so that a stand can be assumed when facing unjustifiably dominant positions. Similarly, other challenges that a noetically oriented research aims to address can also be challenged. In the following, the aim is to present how the first steps in this direction may appear.

4.1   The Practice Knowledge and Orientation Knowledge of Teachers in the Classroom from the Phenomenological Noetic Perspective

From the noetic perspective the processes of knowledge generation are analyzed along with the already generated knowledge structures by *going behind* (noematic) concepts.

The following ten characteristics of "excellent teaching", according to Hilbert MEYER (2004), state such a noematically given knowledge ("noema"). These characteristics, which are usually interpreted in terms of technical as well as interdisciplinary personal, social and methodological competences are a "climate beneficial to learning", "individual development", "sense-making through communication", a "clear structuring", "smart practice", "clarity of content", "transparent performance expectations", "methodological diversity", a "prepared environment" and a "high proportion of real learning time".

Here the question is raised, how can one judge when (and how) these characteristics are given, and when not. We may wonder, how the criteria are related to the instability of learning situations. It is also unclear, how far a relation between the individual and the object and/or social group can be brought about in a controlled manner, if it is not to be enforced. It cannot even be determined uniformly and universally whether or not instructional communication and evaluation processes have a meaning[325] for the different persons involved. In relation

---

325   The "meaning of pedagogical interaction in the classroom" is unterstood here in the sense of William WITTENBRUCH (2010, p. 237, transl. by A.K.) as "[…] the communication between teachers and learners in particular at any action moments of teaching (objectives, starting position, mediation variables, etc.)".

to pedagogical situations, the characteristics of "excellent teaching" can therefore be accused of being distant to context, practices and experience; they might even lead to conflicts, when they label specific teaching situations without taking the possibility that the opposite could be applicable into account. The provided criteria of "excellent teaching" can therefore only be seen as a categorical knowledge that is internalized to a certain extent, not always consciously, in the interaction of the actors, in addition to other forms and formats of an orientative and practical knowledge.

Now, education can only be considered in terms of tension fields that are especially pronounced in school contexts and even significant for them. The challenge of analyzing such tensions arises for the pedagogues (in school), as well as in the reference disciplines of school pedagogy and in teacher education.[326] As we have seen, it is mostly a matter of differentiating normatively between the types of contradictions, antinomies, paradoxes and dilemmata occurring in educational pratices, so that their educational benefit and disadvantages are taken into account.[327] In terms of the tension fields of pedagogy and in relation to professional action taking place under time pressure and under the conditions of polyvalent normativity, an explicit side of pedagogy is always faced with its "tacit" moments.

Seen praxeologically, an educatively framed tutoring is not primarily concerned with *teaching* certain contents to pupils. Moreover, the aim is to give a structure and support to learning processes by an introduction of culture techniques and knowledge bases, by demonstrating different modes of problem solving as well as by the targeted application of materials in teaching. The responsibility of the teacher is to encourage individual pupils for learning, to communicate and structure learning contents. The teachers guide targeted exercises and explain or clarify their performance expectations to the pupils. It is often difficult to determine to what extent they succeed and which other factors will further come into play. It is the responsibility of the teacher to capture and influence the interaction of the respective conditions as carefully as possible. In principle, everything can be employed as a learning impulse. The teachers are left to fend for themselves in the analysis of what is effective as a learning impulse in a given situation. Their experience and orientation knowledge is adjoined by diverse uncertainties.

In this sense, teachers *decide* qua their own actions and judgment about "excellent teaching". The *assessment* of "excellent teaching" of a teacher is the more reliable the more their "finding" ingeniousness is pronounced with respect to an illustration of a concrete learning situation.

---

326 Cf. ESSLINGER-HINZ et al. 2007
327 Cf. STOJANOV 2004

Before providing a more detailed presentation of the possibilities of establishing an experience and orientation knowledge that is relevant to school education, the always associated uncertainties will be brought to attention in the following.

Bernd HACKL (2009) points out that and how the modes of professional acting can be seen as a product of the specifics of the experience of non-knowledge and the resulting impairment of action.[328] Hereby, he opens up a possibility of their visualization and exploration. Based in her/his experience of a particular impairment, a professional with a certain orientative and practical knowledge will be able to identify the roots of a problem. For example, a self-contradictory decision situation is composed differently from the situational impairment of an intended action. The problems associated with a current impairment of the power of disposal are rather different from those deriving from the not fully enlightened premises of a situation.

With respect to each given problem, a teacher will probably draw analogies to similar cases, they will determine possible causes and try to anticipate possible developments with the aim of finding a solution for the particular case. This is usually a reflexively-concomitant, but largely implicit search movement, from which (and this sometimes takes place at lightning speed) the correct assessment of the situation may result. The empirical evidence that a solution of a problem is found, and thus a (new) orientation is obtained is, according to HACKL (2009), the moment of subjectively felt relief. In terms of dealing with imponderables with the aim of subjective relief, he presents the following, empirically verifiable functions: "unlearning" (1), a "reverse thrust" (2), the "readiness to assume risk" (3), habituation (4) and the intuitive use of a body of meanings (5). With respect to Bernhard WALDENFELS (2004b), being "finding in dealing with the unfamiliar" (6) can further be added to the list:

1) "Unlearning": for the solution of a problem, or in terms of attaining new knowledge one must often refrain from already established ways of thinking and modes of action (see above);
2) "Reverse impulse towards change": the emotional-rational orientation in the non-satisfactory, because a precarious here and now is redirected into a reverse impulse towards change, such as toward a memory or expectation;

---

328 In face of HACKL's (2009) argument it should be said that the fact that a professional detects a problem quickly, can also be connected to intractable acting.

3) "Readiness to assume risk": "The recurring experience of successful new beginnings [scil. should be] concentrated in a general attitude of *readiness to assume risk* [accentuation by B. H.]"[329];
4) "Habituation": In solving problems we resort to such sedimentary and habitualised, motor and sensory action patterns that cannot possibly be explicitly remembered or named. An example of this is language: we can speak fluently only, because we do not consider each sentence, how it is constructed; Talk is (just like a "familiarity trap") a habit;
5) In the intuitive recourse, for example, to symbolic representations (such as literature, plans or sketches), everyday objects (such as tools, furniture) and social constellations (such as project groups, school classes) action-relevant meanings may arise. In the sharing of such meanings and in her/his access to these an individual participates in social communities and in the relevant knowledge formats;
6) Being "finding in dealing with the unfamiliar": according to WALDENFELS (2004b), it is our "finding" ingenousness as a spontaneous and reflection-concomitant bodily capacity that captures the phenomena in their qualitative differences, which purely rationally present themselves as dilemmata, disjunctions, as not recoverable foreignness.

Even if all of these functions also have a more or less spontaneous nature, they are still visible in the course of actions, or can respectively be described by the actor. However, in order of coming into view the usual flow of thought must be interrupted, or "obliquely" diverted (see above).

Situations that have led to a redirection, or even re-orientation are often remembered for a long time. As remembered, such conversions and re-orientations can, under certain circumstances, be transferred to reflexive knowledge. Thus, for example, (cherished) habits, as well as the modes of unlearning of supposedly secure knowledge and thrust-reversal, can be identified and questioned by using biographical material. The "readiness to assume risk" and being "finding in dealing with the unfamiliar" can be articulated. Furthermore, knowledge formats such as symbolic representations, everyday objects and social constellations form an in parts "tacit" knowledge base, which is in Educational Sciences currently developed e.g. in a research on things, architecture and cultural phenomena. This research area is not to be underestimated in its significance for modelling school learning.

---

[329] HACKL 2009, p. 76, transl. by A.K.; in German: "die wiederkehrende Erfahrung erfolgreicher Neuanfänge [scil. sollte sich] zu einer generellen Haltung lernender *Risikobereitschaft* [Hervorh. durch B.H.] verdichten"

The broad theme of knowledge formats (see above) cannot be investigated in further detail here. It should be noted that knowledge formats are generated not only in the context of strategies and techniques that are necessary for everyday business, but rather generated multimodally and in all social and cultural fields. The implicitly effective factors in school (such as voice, aspects of attention, improvisation, habitus etc.) are especially researched in the context of anthropological approaches[330]; especially Cultural Science approaches provide valuable templates for these factors.

Knowledge formats can evolve from speaking, or narration modes and speech gestures.[331] Accents are set and meanings are conveyed not only through the modulation of voice and intonation, through pauses and exclamation accents, also narration modes produce certain knowledge formats. Narration modes like the authorial comment, fiction, report, observation etc. can be used not only as an interpretive screen for teaching analysis. They can also be practised and criticized within teacher education.

School education is per se an event of difference,[332] and a teacher can principally reflect her/his own actions in the complex educational field only in the mode of universal humanity in its various manifestations. With reference to MERLEAU-PONTY ([1945] 2005) the fundamental differences between the ways of thinking of children and adults and the similarities have already been interpreted. According to Karl GRAMMER (1988), in the interactions of children and teenagers with adults a reduction of complexity and a predictability of the actions are of primary interest; he writes: "Children are social engineers. They devote most of their time trying to maintain relationships in a positive and in a negative sense."[333] However, this is by no means synonymous with the production of a truly viable social structure. According to GRAMMER (1988), the efforts of children for a social structure focus primarily on reduced complexity and predictability; the possible consequences and constraints that are perceived by adults often play an unimportant role. Social efforts of a child often do not fit to the expectations of their fellow men toward interpersonal relationships (such as discretion). A basic concern of children lies in social relationships that are strongly oriented toward presence.[334]

---

330 Cf. WULF 1997; BERGSTEDT et al. 2012.
331 Cf. DIETRICH 2010
332 Key term: "pedagogy of diversity" (PRENGEL 1993)
333 GRAMMER 1988, p. 302
334 Cf. HONIG 1999

At the same time pupils often have much more differentiated views, for example on school and teaching, than adults expect of them.[335] Confrontational situations in which phenomena of heterogeneity play differently weighted roles would often result from an underestimation of the interpretative activities of pupils by their teachers. GRAMMER (1988) notes that the apparently real concerns of children find very limited consideration in today's education in general. He points out that in principle conflicts that are based on different existing intentions in a group of people are not resolved in the inter-subjective world of adults although they are being directed into socially recognized paths (think of institutions, social structures, laws, etc.). Children perceive conflicts of all kinds differently from adults. It is astonishing that there is hardly any scientific knowledge about this. Since, from a praxeological viewpoint, different ways of dealing with an existing conflict are always to be expected, it is necessary to take into account the perspectives of different persons, including those of children, in relation to one and the same thing. In terms of methodology, the phenomenological approach can be useful for this aim. In educational contexts the different perspectives also have to be coordinated. How this is achieved practically is, as we have seen, an important subject of Children's Studies.

Children's Studies, Pupil Research and Research on Didactics still have great desiderata in this respect. From their point of view, a path must be paved in a certain manner for every kind of knowledge format that is presented as new to a learner; – Rüdiger RHEIN (2010, p. 43 f.) writes about scientific concepts in general: "The inherent rationality of a research and insight process cannot be directly equated with the understanding of this rationality – first of all the way to this rationality must be paved and this requires cognitive-rational, emotional and even physical conditions on behalf of the learner [scil. here, pupils and teacher students, A.K.]." Difficulties that are generally related to learning processes have already been discussed above.

Not only teachers, but also pupils and teacher students are faced with very pronounced heterogenous normativity. As part of the "pupil's job" this possibly appears in the form of possibly strongly conflicting role expectations. So the standpoints, behavior and habits of pupils are simultaneously aimed at the creation of a pupil role and the profiling as a peer. Children or teenagers also justify themselves in front of their parents, relatives or other adults, in certain cases, they also already prove themselves in the labor market. Becoming aware of the diversity of these perspectives could be a goal of teaching. So far, a handling of these different roles is simply passed on to the pupil. It seems that in many respects the demands of

---

335 Cf. BREIDENSTEIN & JERGUS 2005

the pupils on teaching as well as their ways of thinking are often contradictory to what adults mean by "excellent teaching". Thus, to avoid a neglecting of the pupils, in this paradigm the question must be asked to what extent pupils can explicitly recognize and assess (or learn to assess) the qualities of "excellent teaching". This question is not only related to the development of teaching, but also to teacher education.

A central and well to some extent evidently attainable goal of teaching is to convince the pupils of the necessary communication structure for "excellent teaching"; they should realize that an excellent teaching job is rewarding for them. After naming a number of necessary social skills for the task of a "social structure formation" in a class, Karl-Oswald BAUER (2002) draws the following conclusion,: "Educational action becomes professional only when an action repertoire is employed in a specific way, namely on the basis of a substitutional interpretation of the situation of learners."[336] A viable social structure is decisive for a reliable and regulated interaction with each other. In order to establish and maintain such an interaction, a teacher must have knowledge of the various (typical) forms of action and of the learning actions of the pupils. Familiarity with the typical interactions in a group of pupils and with the common patterns of interaction between them and their adult teachers is decisive for the desired course of education and the teaching processes.[337]

According to BOHNSACK (2003, 2005), the possibility of an empirical access to implicit orientation patterns is dependent on the determination of the *how* of the professional decision-making of teachers. The orientative and practical knowledge of a teacher becomes apparent when s/he makes the lesson topic and the learning objectives transparent by explaining the various possible approaches to a certain topic and the peculiarities of learning and communication processes connected with them. Normative orientations and typifications are used in certain contexts. They become evident by the clarification of (actually taken or viable) learning paths by the teacher, her/his distinctions between productive ways and dead ends, by the explanations of learning outcomes, by enabling the access of pupils to specific topics, etc. This is the case for example when a teacher places the statements of pupils, parents or colleagues in certain meaningful contexts, when s/he understands the logic of a statement and gives others the opportunity to communicatively unfold their own relevance systems.

---

336 BAUER 2002, p. 20
337 Cf. BREIDENSTEIN & JERGUS 2005

For this, the "social structure formation" is always demanded by the inescapable anthropological fact of human differences.[338] In particular, the views of pupils on school depend on their heterogeneous starting points for learning (i.e. age, gender, etc., see above) and they also differ fundamentally from those of adults. The plurivalent normativity in the teaching profession implies an entire range of possible attitudes toward and interpretations of these differences as well as different forms of treatment.

The central importance of difference within educational processes finds sufficiently detailed application in educational concepts which start from the hypothesis of a cultural and historical contingency of human life, or in those which build on ideas of a decentered subjectivity.[339] In addition, difference is a principle of scientific knowledge. It can be assumed that in principle teacher trainees and teachers can recognize facets of the (for them inescapable) imponderables "strange" or "foreign"[340] only, if they have a broad anthropological[341] knowledge, also gained within the Cultural Studies. A deep knowledge about institutional, socio-cultural, socio-economic, interactional and intrapsychic events and effects of difference goes along with a broad repertoire of appropriate action and experience knowledge. This should be accompanied by research practices in which especially the forms of interpersonal difference are explored, which are suspended in the "familiarity traps". In particular, the "subjective theories" of the practitioners can be, or contain "familiarity traps". In this way, foreign or self-imposed norms (e.g. of interpersonal difference) can promote habitual narrowness. The fact comes into focus here that "familiarity traps" do not always come into sight explicitly; rather, they often produce effects as "tacit"[342] dimensions of pedagogy.

Various forms of "idealized adult communication" and its influences on educational situations play a special role in this respect. Every teacher argues pri-

---

338 Cf. MORROW & RICHARDS 1996 et al.
339 Hans-Christoph KOLLER (1994) e.g. reads from the psychoanalytic theory of Jacques LACAN's the educational concept of developing opportunities of symbolic realization from the unconscious desire. Michel FOUCAULT ([1982] 1988) emphasizes education as a process of transformation; Jean-Francois LYOTARD ([1979]1984) accentuates the acceptance of foreignness. Similarily, BENNER (2005), KOKEMOHR (2007), ZIRFAS (1999) or MEYER-DRAWE (2007) develop interpretations of the understanding of education, which focus on foreignness.
340 For the topic of "foreignness" cf. the many publications by Bernhard WALDENFELS.
341 The paradigm of historical cultural anthropology examines transformations of human body concepts in changing historical and cultural contexts. (Cf. WULF 1997, WULF & ZIRFAS 2004)
342 POLANYI 1962, 1966 and 1969. Cf. BERGSTEDT et al. 2012.

marily as an adult. HERZOG & VON FELTEN (2001) propose the "idealized adults communication" as the primary theoretical starting point for a reflection and an empirical research of educational action. It should be noted that the decisions of a teacher in an actual classroom situation as well as their analysis a posteriori rather follows the narrative (e.g. given by scenic images and analyzing transfers) than the logical style of thinking. In case of a "familiarity trap" a narrative can be rewritten, so that a it loses its inevitability.

Teachers usually address the difficulties arising from the differences and oppositions in communication of the pupils in the classroom. They usually do this in view of the respective individual development ability that appears plausible to them. This is, inter alia, dependent on psychological, social and socio-cultural factors as well as on the learning level already reached in each case. ZIRFAS (2010, p. 59 with reference to DERRIDA) writes pointedly: "One must decide (pedagogically) in a situation that represents the impossibility of a just decision."[343] An educator takes the responsibility primarily by being aware of this dilemma, indicating where it comes from and, if necessary, resolving it, enduring it and making it understandable to the learner. S/he also has to take into account other instances that are normative for her/his pedagogical decisions. For this purpose, Hans-Georg GADAMER's ([1960] 1989) concept of "phronesis"[344] can be used: With the emphasis on the "being-in-the-world", which is antecedent to our theoretical approach, the "phronesis" is understood as a capacity for insight that is aligned to specific situations. Such a practice-aligned form of insight has its own rationality, which can neither be reduced to rules nor be taught directly. It is always directed at a specific case.

Types of effect and appearance of a "phronesis" can be elicited in the context of a research on educational practices. Especially, teachers are faced with action and time pressure in front of the social group entrusted to them. This is different from the time pressure in other professional fields in so far as a non-compliance with time constraints in the teaching profession is in most cases more difficult to objectively comprehend. The ancient Greeks referred to the creation of a desired

---

343 In German: "Man muss sich (pädagogisch) entscheiden in einer Situation, die die Unmöglichkeit einer gerechten Entscheidung darstellt."
344 "Phronesis" (Ancient Greek: φρόνησις) is in the Aristotelian ethics (Book IV, Nicomachean Ethics) distinguished from other words for wisdom and intellectual virtues. "Phronesis" is the virtue of practical thought and wisdom. It is the ability to judge and act in a situation at hand with reference to ethical values, while neither the abstract knowledge (Ancient Greek: ἐπιστήμη) nor practical or personal benefits are of primary importance but the adequacy of a decision regarding the case at hand.

favorable (further) development[345] of conditions in terms of a temporal, spatial, factual and personal constellation as a "kairos"[346]. "Kairos" is used to describe an (unexpected) event which triggers astonishment, consternation, or other affections; here something occurs that touches and engages us;[347] at the same time the "kairos" also opens up options for action. "Kairoi" as the perceptions of the favorable moments for certain educational and instructional activities by the teacher can be described as the cause of "excellent teaching". However, the perception of learning opportunities is also required from the pupil. Such auspicious occasions can be observed and described.

An important goal of practice research and of science-oriented educational experience is thus to identify the factors that are beneficial is learning processes and at the same time effective in the classroom. Such factors should enable aim-oriented decisions in complex situations and under time pressure and thus relieve the teacher. The listed aspects of education and teaching practice show that learning and teaching processes do not solely rely on unerring and rational control, but also crucially on "tacit" knowledge. In its relevance to the stimulation of learning and educational processes or to the development of skills, the process character of this practice and orientation knowledge should be the focus of analytical attention of school pedagogy and teacher education. Phenomenological, performativity-theoretical and praxeological pedagogical practice research provides valuable references for teacher education. This applies not only thematically but also in terms of methodology. Thematically, the Cultural Studies and anthropologically-oriented approaches are of great importance for teacher education, especially in terms of the exploration of interpersonal and other differential events.

---

345 Joseph WALTERS & Howard GARDNER (1986) describe the "crystallizing experience" as the willingness to discover the talents and potentials of another person. This willingness should always be shown to children.

346 Ancient Greek καιρός, the right moment, the right place.

347 MERSCH 2002, p. 13–30; cf. also the concept of responsitivity of Bernhard WALDENFELS and the performative paradigm (both, see below).

References

Achatz, M.; Tippelt, R. (2001): Wandel von Erwerbsarbeit und Begründungen kompetenzorientierten Lernens im internationalen Kontext. In: Bolder, A.; Heinz, W. R.; Kutscha, G. (eds.): Deregulierung der Arbeit – Pluralisierung der Bildung? (Jahrbuch Bildung und Arbeit; 1999/2000). Opladen: Leske + Budrich, 111–127

Aden, M.; Peters, M. (2012): ‚Standart' – Möglichkeiten, Grenzen und die produktive Erweiterung kompetenzorientierter Standards in performativen Prozessen der Kunstpädagogik. Hamburg, Köln, Oldenburg: University Press.

Adorno, T.W.; Horkheimer, M. ([1944] 1988): Dialektik der Aufklärung, Frankfurt/Main: S. Fischer

Aptheker, B. (1989): Tapestries of Life. Women's Work, Women's Consciousness, and the Meaning of Daily Experience. Amherst: The University of Massachusetts Press

Arendt, H. ([1958] 1998): The Human Condition. Chicago, London: The University of Chicago Press

Ariès, Ph. (1962): Centuries of Childhood. New York: Vintage Books

Aristotle (2004): Nicomachean Ethics (transl. and ed. by Roger Crisp), Book IV. Cambridge: Cambridge University Press

Asmuth, C. (2006). Authentizität und Konstruktion. Körperbegriffe zwischen historischer Relativität und unmittelbarer Gegenwärtigkeit. In: Antje Stache (ed.): Das Harte und das Weiche. Körper – Erfahrung – Konstruktion. Bielefeld: Transcript Verlag, 119–142

Austin, J.-L. (1975): How to Do Things with Words. The William James Lectures delivered at Harvard University in 1955. Oxford: Clarendon Press

Bachelard, G. ([1938] 2004): La formation de l'esprit scientifique. Paris: Vrin, Collection Bibliothèque d'histoire de la philosophie

Bachelard, G. ([1943] 1990): L'air et les songes. Essai sur l'imagination du mouvement. Paris: José Corti

Bachelard, G. ([1957] 1998): La poétique de l'espace. Paris: Presses Universitaires de France, Collection Quadrige grands textes

Bachelard, G. (1971): Epistémologie. Textes choisies. Paris: P.U.F

Bauer, K.-O. (2002): Vom Allroundtalent zum Professional – Was bedeutet Lehrerprofessionalisierung heute? In: Pädagogik 54/11, 18–22

Beck, K. (1983): Lehrerausbildung als Verbindung von Theorie und Praxis? Über den Status von Theorien im Kontext der Lehrerrolle. In: Pädagogische Rundschau 37/2, 145–169

Beck, U.; Bonß, W. (eds.) (1989): Weder Sozialtechnologie noch Aufklärung? Analysen zur Verwendung sozialwissenschaftlichen Wissens. Frankfurt/Main: Suhrkamp

Benner, D. (ed.) (2005): Zeitschrift für Pädagogik. 49. Beiheft: Erziehung – Bildung – Negativität. Theoretische Annäherungen. Analysen zum Verhältnis von Macht und Negativität. Exemplarische Studien. Weinheim, Basel: Beltz

Benner, D.; Englisch, A. (2005): Einführung. Über pädagogisch relevante und erziehungswissenschaftlich fruchtbare Aspekte der Negativität menschlicher Erfahrung. In: Benner, D. (ed.): Zeitschrift für Pädagogik. 49. Beiheft: Erziehung – Bildung – Negativität. Theoretische Annäherungen. Analysen zum Verhältnis von Macht und Negativität. Exemplarische Studien. Weinheim, Basel: Beltz, 7–23

Bergstedt, B.; Herbert, A.; Kraus, A.; Wulf, Ch. (eds.) (2012): Tacit Dimensions of Pedagogy. Münster, New York, München, Berlin: Waxmann

Bilstein, J.; Dornberg, B.; Kneip, W. (eds.) (2007): Curriculum des Unwägbaren. I. Ästhetische Bildung im Kontext von Schule und Kultur. Oberhausen: Athena

Blömeke, S. (1998): Reform der Lehrer(innen)bildung? Zentren für Lehrer(innen)bildung: Bestandsaufnahme, Konzepte, Beispiele. Bad Heilbrunn/Obb.: Klinkhardt

Bloom, B.S. (1973): Taxonomie von Lernzielen im kognitiven Bereich. Weinheim, Basel: Beltz

Blumenthal, J. von (2005): Governance – eine kritische Zwischenbilanz. Zeitschrift für Politikwissenschaft 15/4, 1149–1180

Böhle, F.; Pfeiffer, S.; Sevsay-Tegethoff, N. (eds.) (2004): Die Bewältigung des Unplanbaren. Wiesbaden: VS Verlag für Humanwissenschaften

Böhme, J. (2004): Qualitative Schulforschung auf Konsolidierungskurs. In: Helsper, W.; Böhme, J. (eds.): Handbuch der Schulforschung. Wiesbaden: VS Verlag, 125–155

Bohnsack, R. (2003): Rekonstruktive Sozialforschung. Einführung in qualitative Methoden. Opladen

Bohnsack, R. (2005): Standards nicht-standardisierter Forschung in den Erziehungs- und Sozialwissenschaften. In: Zeitschrift für Erziehungswissenschaft, 8. Jahrgang, Beiheft 4, 63–81

Bohnsack, R. (2007): Performativität, Performanz und dokumentarische Methode. In: Wulf, C.; Zirfas, J. (eds.): Pädagogik des Performativen. Theorien, Methoden, Perspektiven. Weinheim, Basel: Beltz, 200–212

Bonß, W. (2003): "Bildung" in der (Arbeits-)und "Wissensgesellschaft". In: Lindner, W.; Thole, W.; Weber, J. (eds.): Kinder- und Jugendarbeit als Bildungsprojekt. Opladen: Leske & Budrich, 11–31

Bonß, W.; Hohlfeld, R.; Kollek, R. (eds.) (1993): Wissenschaft als Kontext – Kontexte der Wissenschaft, Hamburg: Junius Verlag

Bos, W.; Pietsch, M.; Poerschke, J.; Vieluf, U. (2007): Zusammenfassung wichtiger Ergebnisse zu Kompetenzen und Einstellungen von Hamburger Schülerinnen und Schülern. In: Bos, W.; Pietsch, M. (eds.): KESS 4 – Kompetenzen und Einstellungen von Schülerinnen und Schülern am Ende der Jahrgangsstufe 4 in Hamburger Grundschulen. Münster, New York, München, Berlin: Waxmann, 1–8

Bourdieu, P. ([1972] 1977): Outline of a Theory of Practice. Cambridge: Cambridge University Press
Bourdieu, P. ([1980] 1998): Practical Reason. On the Theory of Action. Stanford, California: Stanford University Press
Bourdieu, P. ([2002] 2009): For an *Engaged* Knowledge. Available at: http://www.inter mediamfa.org/imd501/index.php?pg=blog&post_id=257 [latest access: 10.03.2015]
Bowman, V. (ed.) (2007): Scholarly Resources for Children and Childhood Studies: A Research Guide and Annotated Bibliography. Lanham, MD: Scarecrow Press
Bramberger, A. (2007): Identifizierungen. Geschlechtersensible Pädagogik und radikale Performativität. In: Wulf, Ch.; Zirfas, J. (eds.): Pädagogik des Performativen. Theorien, Methoden, Perspektiven. Weinheim, Basel: Beltz, 101–109
Breidenstein, G. (2006): Teilnahme am Unterricht. Ethnographische Studien zum Schülerjob. Wiesbaden: VS Verlag
Breidenstein, G. (2008): Allgemeine Didaktik und praxeologische Unterrichtsforschung. In: Meyer, M.A.; Prenzel, M.; Hellekamps, S. (eds.): Perspektiven der Didaktik. Zeitschrift für Erziehungswissenschaft. Sonderheft 9. Wiesbaden: VS Verlag für Sozialwissenschaften, 201–218
Breidenstein, G.; Jergus, K. (2005): Schule als "Job"? Beobachtungen aus der achten Klasse. In: Breidenstein, G.; Prengel, A. (eds.): Schulforschung und Kindheitsforschung – ein Gegensatz? Wiesbaden: VS-Verlag, 177–199
Breidenstein, G.; Kelle, H. (1999): Kinder als Akteure: Ethnographische Ansätze in der Kindheitsforschung. In: Zeitschrift für Soziologie der Erziehung und Sozialisation, 16, 47–67
Brentano, F. (1982): Deskriptive Psychologie. Hamburg: Meiner
Breuer, F. (1995): Das Selbstkonfrontations-Interview als Forschungsmethode. In: König, E.; Zedler, P. (eds.): Bilanz qualitativer Forschung. Band II: Methoden. Weinheim: Deutscher Studienverlag, 159–182
Bromme, R. (1992): Der Lehrer als Experte. Zur Psychologie des professionellen Wissens. Bern: Huber
Butler; J. (1990): Gender Trouble: Feminism and the Subversion of Identity. London, New York: Routledge
Carlgren, I. (2012): Kunskap för bildning? In: Englund, T.; Forsberg, E.; Sundberg, D. (eds.): Vad räknas som kunskap? Läroplansteoretiska utsikter och inblickar i lärarutbildning och skola. Stockholm: Liber, 118–139
Christensen, P.; James, A. (eds.) (2008): Research with Children. Perspectives and Practices. New York u.a.: Routledge
Combe, A.; Kolbe, F.-U. (2004): Lehrerprofessionalität: Wissen, Können, Handeln. In: Helsper, W.; Böhme, J. (eds.): Handbuch der Schulforschung. Wiesbaden: VS Verlag, 833–851
Comenius, J.A. ([1657] 1896): The Great Didactic. The Whole Art of Teaching All Things to Men. London: Adam and Charles Black

Council of the European Union (2007): Improving the Quality of Teacher Education. Available at: http://europa.eu/legislation_summaries/education_training_youth/lifelong_ learning/c11101_en.htm [latest access: 10.03.2015]

Dahlberg, G.; Moss, P.; Pence, A. (2002): Från kvalité till meningskapande. Stockholm: HLS Förlag

De Mause, L. (1974): The History of Childhood. New York: Harper & Row

Deckert-Peaceman, H.; Dietrich, C.; Stenger, U. (2010): Einführung in die Kindheitsforschung. Darmstadt: Wissenschaftliche Buchgesellschaft

Deleuze, G. ([1968] 1994): Difference and Repetition. New York: Columbia University Press

Deleuze, G.; Guattari, F. ([1991] 1994): What Is Philosophy? New York: Columbia University Press

Derrida, J. ([1967] 1978): Writing and Difference. London, New York: Routledge

Derrida, J. (1989): Some Statements and Truisms about Neologisms, Newisms, Positisms, Parasitisms, and other small Seismisms, The States of Theory. New York: Columbia University Press

Derrida, J. ([1998] 2002): The University without Condition. In: Derrida, J.: *Without Alibi*. Stanford: Stanford University Press

Dewe, B. (1997): Grenzen der Didaktik: Über den Hiatus zwischen Lehrerwissen und Lehrerkönnen. In: Keuffer, J.; Meyer, A. M. (eds.): Didaktik und kultureller Wandel. Weinheim, Basel: Beltz, 220–248

Diemer, A. (1964): Was heißt Wissenschaft. Meisenheim am Glan: Hain

Dietrich, C. (2010): Zur Sprache kommen: Sprechgestik in jugendlichen Bildungsprozessen in und außerhalb der Schule. Weinheim: Juventa

Dohmen, G. (2001): Das informelle Lernen. Die internationale Erschließung einer bisher vernachlässigten Grundform menschlichen Lernens für das lebenslange Lernen aller. Bonn: Bundesministerium für Bildung und Forschung (BMBF)

Dreyfus, H.; Dreyfus, S. (1987): Künstliche Intelligenz. Von den Grenzen der Denkmaschine und dem Wert der Intuition. Reinbek b. Hamburg: Rowohlt

Du Bois-Reymond, M.; Sünker, H.; Krüger, H.-H. (eds.) (2001): Childhood in Europe: Approaches, Trends, Findings. New York: Peter Lang.

Eder, F.; Altrichter, H. (2009): Qualitätsentwicklung und Qualitätssicherung im österreichischen Schulwesen: Bilanz aus 15 Jahren Diskussion und Entwicklungsperspektiven für die Zukunft. In: Specht, W. (ed.): Nationaler Bildungsbericht Österreich 2009. Band 2: Fokussierte Analysen bildungspolitischer Schwerpunktthemen. Graz: Leykam, 305–322

Ehrenspeck, Y.; Rustemeyer, D. (1996): Bestimmt, unbestimmt. In: Combe, A.; Helsper, W. (eds.): Pädagogische Professionalität. Untersuchungen zum Typus pädagogischen Handelns. Frankfurt/Main: Suhrkamp, 368–390

Englund, T.; Forsberg, E.; Sundberg, D. (eds.) (2012): Vad räknas som kunskap? Läroplansteoretiska utsikter och inblickar i lärarutbildning och skola. Stockholm: Liber

Esslinger-Hinz, I.; Unseld, G.; Reinhard-Hauck, P.; Röbe, E.; Fischer, H.-J.; Kust, T.; Däschler-Seiler, S. (eds.) (2007): Guter Unterricht als Planungsaufgabe: Ein Studien- und Arbeitsbuch zur Grundlegung unterrichtlicher Basiskompetenzen. Bad Heilbrunn: Klinkhardt

Esslinger-Hinz, I.; Fischer, H.-J. (eds.) (2008): Spannungsfelder der Erziehung und Bildung. Ein Studienbuch zu grundlegenden Themenfeldern der Pädagogik. Hohengehren: Schneider Verlag

European Commission (2008): The European Qualification Framework for Lifelong Learning. Luxemburg: Office for Official Publications of the European Communities. Available at: http://ec.europa.eu/ploteus/search/site?f%5B0%5D=im_field_entity_type%3A97 [latest access: 10.03.2015]

Faux, R. (2000): A description of the uses of content analyses and interviews in educational/psychological research [29 paragraphs]. Forum: Qualitative Social Research [Online Journal], 1(1). Available at: http://www.qualitative-research.net/fqs-texte/1-00/1-00faux-e.htm [latest access: 10.03.2015]

Feiman-Nemser, S.; Buchmann, M. (1986): The First Year of Teacher Preparation: Transition to Pedagogical Thinking. In: Journal of Curriculum Studies, 18, 239–256

Felten, R. von (2005): Lernen im reflexiven Praktikum. Eine vergleichende Untersuchung. Münster, New York, München, Berlin: Waxmann

Fend, H. (1974): Gesellschaftliche Bedingungen schulischer Sozialisation. Weinheim, Basel: Beltz

Feyerabend, P.K. (1975): Against Method: Outline of an Anarchist Theory of Knowledge. London: New Left Books

Fischer, D.; Friebertshäuser, B.; Kleinau, E. (eds.) (1999): Neues Lehren an der Hochschule. Einblicke und Ausblicke. Weinheim: Deutscher Studienverlag

Fischer, T. (ed.) (2006): Hochschule und Erlebnispädagogik. Hochschuldidaktische Bausteine einer handlungs- und erlebnisorientierten Pädagogik. Baltmannsweiler: Schneider Verlag Hohengehren

Fleck, L. (1980): Entstehung und Entwicklung einer wissenschaftlichen Tatsache. Einführung in die Lehre vom Denkstil und Denkkollektiv. Frankfurt/Main: Suhrkamp

Forster, E. (2007): Radikale Performativität. In: Wulf, Ch.; Zirfas, J. (eds.): Pädagogik des Performativen. Theorien, Methoden, Perspektiven. Weinheim, Basel: Beltz, 224–237

Foucault, M. ([1966] 1970): The Order of Things: An Archaeology of the Human Sciences. New York: Patheon Books

Foucault, M. ([1982] 1988): Technologies of the Self. In: Martin, L.H.; Gutman, H.; Hutton, P.H. (eds.): Technologies on the Self: A Seminar with Michel Foucault. Amherst: The University of Massachusetts Press, 16–49

Frank, I.; Gutschow, K.; Münchhausen, G. (2005): Informelles Lernen. Bielefeld: Bertelsmann

Fredriksson, U. (2006): European teacher education policy: recommendations and indicators. Paper at the 31st Annual Association of Teacher Education Europe (ATEE) Conference 'Co-operative Partnerships in Teacher Education'. Available at: www.pef.uni-lj.si/atee/978-961-6637-06-0/715-723.pdf [latest access: 10.03.2015]

Fredriksson, U.; Hoskins, B. (2007): The Development of Learning to Learn in a European Context. In: The Curriculum Journal 18/2, 127-134

Frey, A. (2006): Methoden und Instrumente zur Diagnose beruflicher Kompetenzen von Lehrkräften – eine erste Standortbestimmung zu bereits publizierten Instrumenten. In: Zeitschrift für Pädagogik. Beiheft 51, 30-46

Friebertshäuser, B.; Prengel, A. (2003): Einleitung: Profil, Intentionen, Traditionen und Inhalte des Handbuches. In: Friebertshäuser, B.; Prengel, A. (eds.): Handbuch Qualitative Forschungsmethoden in der Erziehungswissenschaft. Weinheim, München: Juventa, 11-24

Funke-Wieneke, J. (2004): Bewegungs- und Sportpädagogik. Baltmannsweiler: Schneider

Gadamer, H.-G. (1979): Verlust der sinnlichen Bildung als Ursache des Verlustes von Wertmaßstäben. In: Wichmann, H. (ed.): Der Mensch ohne Hand oder die Zerstörung der menschlichen Ganzheit. München: dtv, 15-28

Gadamer, H.-G. ([1960] 1989): Truth and Method, trans. by J. Weinsheimer and D.G. Marshall. New York: Crossroad

Gadamer, H.-G. ([1993] 2001): Gadamer in Conversation, trans. by R. Palmer, New Haven: Yale University Press

Gebauer, G.; Wulf, Ch. (1998): Spiel – Ritual – Geste. Mimetisches Handeln in der sozialen Welt. Reinbek: Rowohlt

Geertz, C. (1973): The Interpretation of Cultures. New York: Basic Books

Gibbs, G. (2013): Reflections on the Changing Nature of Educational Development. In: International Journal for Academic Development 18:1, 4-14. Available at: http://www.tandfonline.com/doi/pdf/10.1080/1360144X.2013.751691 [14.02.2015]

Goffman, E. (1959): The Presentation of Self in Everyday Life. New York: Doubleday & Company

Grammer, K. (1988): Biologische Grundlagen des Sozialverhaltens. Darmstadt: Wissenschaftliche Buchgesellschaft

Groeben, N. (1988): Explikation des Konstrukts 'Subjektive Theorie'. In: Groeben, N.; Wahl, D.; Schlee, J.; Scheele, B. (eds.): Das Forschungsprogramm Subjektive Theorien. Eine Einführung in die Psychologie des reflexiven Subjekts. Tübingen: Francke, 17-24

Groeben, N.; Scheele, B. (1982): Grundlagenprobleme eines Forschungsprogramms "Subjektive Theorien": Zum Stand der Diskussion. In: Dann, H. D.; Humpert, W.; Krause, F.; Tennstädt, K. C. (eds.): Analyse und Modifikation subjektiver Theorien von Lehrern. Ergebnisse und Perspektiven eines Kolloquiums. Konstanz: Universität, Zentrum I Bildungsforschung, 9-12

Groeben, N.; Wahl, D.; Schlee, J.; Scheele, B. (1988): Das Forschungsprogramm Subjektive Theorien. Eine Einführung in die Psychologie des reflexiven Subjekts. Tübingen: Francke

Groppe, C. (2014, unpublished): Universität als Gegenstand der Erziehungswissenschaft. Analysen zu historischen, aktuellen und zukünftigen Entwicklungen der deutschen Universität. Keynote at the Congress of DGfE 2014 'Traditionen & Zukünfte' at the Humboldt University Berlin

Gruntz-Stoll, J. (1999): Erziehung, Unterricht, Widerspruch. Pädagogische Antinomien und Paradoxe Anthropologie. Bern: Lang

Hackl, B. (2006): Ohne Worte. Über Sinn, Sprache und Domestizierung des Körpers. In: Heinrich, M.; Greiner, U. (eds.): Schauen was 'rauskommt. Kompetenzführung, Evaluation und Systemsteuerung im Bildungswesen. Münster: LIT-Verlag, 241–266

Hackl, B. (2008): Was geschieht in der Schule? Überlegungen zur Erforschung der verborgenen Dimensionen des Unterrichts. In: Eder, F.; Hörl, G. (eds.): Gerechtigkeit und Effizienz im Bildungswesen, Unterricht, Schulentwicklung und Lehrerinnenbildung als professionelle Handlungsfelder. Wien: LIT-Verlag, 73–95

Hackl, B. (2009): Gefühle der Veränderung. Die Bedeutung der Emotionen in einem nicht-intellektualistischen Lernverständnis. In: Esterbauer, R.; Rinofner, S. (eds.): Emotionen – Im Spannungsfeld von Phänomenologie und Wissenschaften. Frankfurt/Main: Peter Lang, 69–91

Haraway, D. (1988): Situated Knowledges: The Science Question in Feminism and the Privilege of Partial Perspective. In: Feminist Studies, 14/3, 575–599

Haraway, D. (1991): Simians, Cyborgs, and Women: The Reinvention of Nature. London, New York: Routledge

Haraway, D. (1997): Modest_Witness@Second_Millennium. FemaleMan©_Meets_ OncoMouse™. Feminism and Technoscience. London, New York: Routledge

Haraway, D. (2000): HOW Like a Leaf. An Interview with Thyrza Nichols Goodeve. London, New York: Routledge

Harding, S. (1991): Whose Science? Whose Knowledge? Thinking from Women's Lives. Buckingham: Open University Press

Hattie, J. (2008): Visible Learning. A Synthesis of Over 800 Meta-Analyses Relating to Achievement. Abington: Routledge

Hauptmeier, G. (1980): Verfahrensweisen der didaktischen Reduktion. Möglichkeiten einer unterrichtspraktischen Umsetzung. In: Die Deutsche Berufs- und Fachschule 76/11, 820–834

Hausendorf, H. (2001): Was ist 'altersgemäßes Sprechen?' Empirische Anmerkungen am Beispiel des Erzählens und Zuhörens zwischen Kindern und Erwachsenen. In: Osnabrücker Beiträge zur Sprachtheorie 61, 11–33

Heid, H. (2013): Werteerziehung – ohne Werte!? Beitrag zur Erörterung ihrer Voraussetzungen. In: Zeitschrift für Pädagogik 59/2, 238–257

Heinrich, K. (1981): Tertium datur: eine religionsphilosophische Einführung in die Logik. Basel, Frankfurt/Main: Stroemfeld/Roter Stern

Heinzel, F. (ed.) (2000): Methoden der Kindheitsforschung. Ein Überblick über Forschungszugänge zur kindlichen Perspektive. Weinheim, München: Juventa

Helsper, W.; Hörster, R.; Kade, J. (eds.) (2003): Ungewissheit. Pädagogische Felder im Modernisierungsprozess. Weilerswist: Velbrück Wissenschaft

Hentig, H. von (1993): Die Schule neu: Eine Übung in pädagogischer Vernunft. München, Wien: Hanser

Herbart, J.F. ([1802] 1969): Zwei Vorlesungen über Pädagogik. In: Kehrbach, K.; Flügel, O. (eds.): Sämtliche Werke, Bd. 1. Aalen: Scientia. 279–290

Herbart, J.F. (1837): Lehrbuch zur Einleitung in die Philosophie. Königsberg: August Wilhem Unzer

Hericks, U.; Kunze, I. (2004): Forschung zu Didaktik und Curriculum. In: Helsper, W.; Böhme, J. (eds.): Handbuch der Schulforschung. Wiesbaden: VS Verlag, 721–752

Herzog, W. (1995): Forschungs- und Entwicklungsprojekte der Konferenz der Lehrerbildungsinstitutionen. Abstracts zum Forschungstag 1995. Bern: Konferenz der Lehrerbildungsinstitutionen

Herzog, W. (2005): Pädagogik und Psychologie im Wörterbuch. Zur Normalität der Erziehungswissenschaft. In: Zeitschrift für Pädagogik 51, 673–693

Herzog, W. (2007): Welche Wissenschaft für die Lehrerinnen- und Lehrer(innen)bildung? In: Beiträge zur Lehrer(innen)bildung. Zeitschrift für Theorie und Praxis der Aus- und Weiterbildung von Lehrerinnen und Lehrern 25 (3), 306–316

Herzog, W.; Felten, R. von (2001): Erfahrung und Reflexion. Zur Professionalisierung der Praktikumsbildung von Lehrerinnen und Lehrern. In: Beiträge zur Lehrer(innen)bildung 19, 17–28

Hinz, A. (1995): Integration und Heterogenität. Available at: bidok.uibk.ac.at/library/hinz-heterogenitaet.html [latest access: 10.03.2015]

Hirschauer, S. (2004): Praktiken und ihre Körper. Über materielle Partizipanden des Tuns. In: Hörning, K.H.; Reuter, J. (eds.): Doing Culture. Neue Positionen zum Verhältnis von Kultur und sozialer Praxis. Bielefeld: Transcript, 73–91

Hoffmann, M. (1999): Problems with Peirce's Concept of Abduction. In: Foundations of Science 4 (3), 271–305

Honig, M.-S. (1999): Entwurf einer Theorie der Kindheit. Frankfurt/Main: Suhrkamp

Hood, C. (1991): A Public Management for All Seasons. Public Administration 69 (Spring), 3–19

Hudson, B. (1999): Seeking connections and searching for meaning: teaching as reflective practice. In: TNTEE Publications 2 (1), October, 37–47

Hudson, B. (2008): Didactic Design for Technology Supported Learning. In: Meyer, M.A.; Prenzel, M.; Hellekamps, S. (eds.): Perspektiven der Didaktik. Zeitschrift für Erziehungswissenschaft. Sonderheft 9, 139–157

Hudson, B.; Meyer, M. (eds.) (2011): Beyond Fragmentation. Didactics, Learning and Teaching. Opladen, Farmington Hills: Barbara Budrich

Hug, Th. (1996): Wissenschaftsforschung als Feldforschung – ein erziehungswissenschaftliches Projekt. In: Störquelle. Zeitschrift für kritische Psychologinnen und Psychologen 8/3, No. 32, 45–63

Humboldt, von W. ([1836] 1999): On Language. On the Diversity of Human Language Construction and Its Influence on the Mental Development of the Human Species. Cambridge: Cambridge University Press

Humboldt, von W. (1903–1920): Gesammelte Schriften: Ausgabe der Preussischen Akademie der Wissenschaften. Vol. I, Berlin: Behr

Husserl, E. ([1931] 1982): Cartesian Meditations. An Introduction to Phenomenology. The Hague, Boston, London: Kluwer

Husserl, E. ([1913] 1983): Ideas Pertaining to a Pure Phenomenology and to a Phenomenological Philosophy. First Book: General Introduction to a Pure Phenomenology. The Hague, Boston, Lancaster: Kluwer

Ingersoll, R. (2003): Who Controls Teachers' Work: Power and Accountability in America's Schools. Cambridge, Massachusetts: Harvard University Press

Jackson, P. W. (1968): Life in Classrooms. New York: Holt, Reinhart & Winston

Jahnke, T.; Meyerhöfer, W. (eds.) (2006): Pisa & Co. Kritik eines Programms. Hildesheim, Berlin: Franzbecker

James, A.; James, A.L. (2008): Key Concepts in Childhood Studies. London: Sage

Joas, H. ([1992] 1996): The Creativity of Action. Chicago, London: The University of Chicago Press

Kagan, D.M. (1992): Professional Growth among Preservice and Beginning Teachers. In: Review of Educational Research 62 (2), 129–169

Kern, I. (1975): Idee und Methode der Philosophie: Leitgedanken für eine Theorie der Vernunft. Berlin, New York: De Gruyter

Ķestere, I.; Ozola, I. (2011): Pedagogy: A Discipline under Diverse Appellations. Baltic Journal of European Studies, vol. 1, no. 1(9), 306–321

Kleist, H. von ([1805/6] 2004): On the Gradual Production of Thought Whilst Speaking. In: von Kleist, H.; Constantine, D. (eds.): Selected Writings. Indianapolis: Hackett Publishing Company, 405–409

Klijn, E. (2012): New Public Management and Governance: A Comparison. In: Levi-Faur, D. (ed.): The Oxford Handbook of Governance. Oxford: Oxford University Press, 201–214

König, E.; Zedler, P. (2002): Theorien der Erziehungswissenschaft. Einführung in Grundlagen, Methoden und praktische Konsequenzen. Weinheim, Basel: Beltz

Kokemohr, R. (2007): Bildung als Selbst- und Weltentwurf im Anspruch des Fremden. In: Koller, H.-C.; Marotzki, W.; Sanders, O. (eds.): Bildungsprozesse und Fremdheitserfahrung. Beiträge zu einer Theorie transformatorischer Bildungsprozesse. Bielefeld: Transcript, 13–68

Kolesch, D. (1999): Performative Turns in den Kulturwissenschaften. Von der Textualität zur Stimmlichkeit? In: Rüsen, J. (ed.): Jahrbuch 1998/1999 des Kulturwissenschaftlichen Instituts in Wissenschaftszentrum NRW. Essen, 254–275

Koller, H.-C. (1994): Bildung als Ab-Bildung? Eine bildungstheoretische Fallstudie im Anschluss an Jacques Lacan. In: Pädagogische Rundschau 48, 687–706

Krämer, S.; Stahlhut, M. (2001): Das Performative als Thema der Sprach- und Kulturphilosophie. In: Fischer-Lichte, E.; Wulf, Ch. (eds.): Paragrana. Internationale Zeitschrift für Historische Anthropologie. Band 10, Heft 1: Theorien des Performativen, 35–64

Kraus, A. (2002): Nihilismus, Sprache und Wahrnehmung. Zur Anthropologie Lacans und Merleau-Pontys, Berlin: Freie Universität, Doctoral Dissertation 2000. Available at: http://www.diss.fu-berlin.de/diss/receive/FUDISS_thesis_000000019380 [latest access: 10.03.2015]

Kraus, A. (2007): Welche Perspektiven könnte eine Kultur-PISA-Studie den musisch-ästhetischen Fächer eröffnen? In: Zeitschrift für Theaterpädagogik. Korrespondenzen 52, 2008, 25–29

Kraus, A. (2010): Einführung. Bildungsprozesse in der Schule. In: Kraus, Anja (ed.): Körperlichkeit in der Schule – Aktuelle Körperdiskurse und ihre Empirie. Vol. III. Oberhausen: Athena Verlag, 7–22

Kraus, A. (2013): On the Relationship between Praxeology and Phenomenology. In: Herbert, A.; Kraus, A. (eds.): Praxeology as a Challenge. Modelling the Tacit Dimensions of Pedagogy. Münster, New York, München, Berlin: Waxmann, 21–30

Kraus, A. (2015): Anforderungen an eine Wissenschaft für die Lehrer(innen)bildung. Wissenschaftstheoretische Überlegungen zur praxisorientierten Lehrer(innen)bildung. Münster, New York: Waxmann

Kron, F.W. (1999): Wissenschaftstheorie für Pädagogen. München, Basel: Reinhardt

Kuhlen, R. (1991): Information and Pragmatic Value Adding: Language Games and Information Science. In: Computers and the Humanities 25/2, 93–101

Kuhn, T.S. (1962): Structure of Scientific Revolutions. Chicago, London: The University of Chicago Press

Lamnek, S. (1995): Qualitative Sozialforschung. Band 2: Methoden und Techniken. Weinheim, Basel: Beltz

Lamprecht, J. (2012): Rekonstruktiv-responsive Evaluation in der Praxis. Neue Perspektiven dokumentarischer Evaluatonsforschung. Wiesbaden: VS Verlag

Lave, J. (1998): Cognition in Practice. Mind, Mathematics and Culture in Everyday Life. Cambridge: Cambridge University Press

Le Doeuff, Michele (1977): Women and Philosophy. In: Radical Philosophy 17, 2–11

Leggewie, C.; Zifonun, D.; Lang, A.; Siepmann, M.; Hoppen, J. (eds.) (2011): Schlüsselwerke der Kulturwissenschaften. Bielefeld: Transkript

Lenzer, G. (2001): Children's Studies: Beginnings and Purposes. In: The Lion and the Unicorn 25. Baltimore: Johns Hopkins University Press, 181–186

Liebau, E. (2003): Schul-Theater. In: Bering, K.; Bilstein, J.; Thurn, H.P. (eds.): Kultur-Kompetenz. Oberhausen: Athena, 420–435

Longino, H.E. (2001): The Fate of Knowledge. Princeton, NJ: Princeton University Press

Löwisch, D.-J. (2000): Kompetentes Handeln. Bausteine für eine lebensweltbezogene Bildung. Darmstadt: Wissenschaftliche Buchgesellschaft

Lyotard, J.-F. ([1979] 1984): The *Postmodern Condition*. Manchester: Manchester University Press

Mach, E. ([1905] 1976): Knowledge and Error: Sketches on the Psychology of Enquiry. Boston: Reidel

Manen, M. van (1995): Herbart und der Takt im Unterricht. In: Zeitschrift für Pädagogik 33. Beiheft, 61–80

Mannheim, K. (1936): Ideology and Utopia. New York: Harcourt, Brace and World

Masschelein, J.; Ricken, N. (2003): Do we (still) need the concept of Bildung? In: Educational Philosophy and Theory 35/2, 139–154

Mauss, M. (1974): Oeuvres. Vol. 2: Représentations collectives et diversité de civilisations. Présentation de Victor Karady. Paris: Éditions de Minuit

Mayr, J.; Neuweg, G.H. (2006): Der Persönlichkeitsansatz in der Lehrer(innen)forschung. Grundsätzliche Überlegungen, exemplarische Befunde und Implikationen für die Lehrer(innen)bildung. In: Greiner, U.; Heinrich, M. (eds.): Schauen, was 'rauskommt. Kompetenzförderung, Evaluation und Systemsteuerung im Bildungswesen. Wien: Lit-Verlag, 183–206

Mayr, J.; Paseka, A. (2002): "Lehrerpersönlichkeit". Journal für Lehrer-und Lehrerinnenbildung 2/2, 50–55

Meder, N. (1996): Der Sprachspieler. Ein Bildungskonzept für die Informationsgesellschaft. In: Vierteljahresschrift für wissenschaftliche Pädagogik 71, 145–162

Merleau-Ponty, M. ([1964] 1968): The Visible and the Invisible. Trans. by Alphonso Lingis. Evanston: Northwestern University Press

Merleau-Ponty, M. ([1961] 1993): Eye and Mind. Trans. by Michael Smith in: The Merleau-Ponty Aesthetics Reader ed. by Galen Johnson & Michael Smith. Evanston: Northwestern University Press, 121–149

Merleau-Ponty, M. ([1945] 2005): Phenomenology of Perception. London: Taylor and Francis e-Library

Mersch, D. (2002): Ereignis und Aura. Untersuchungen zu einer Ästhetik des Performativen. Frankfurt/Main: Suhrkamp

Meyer, C. (2003): Inszenierung ästhetischer Erfahrungsräume. Ein Beitrag zur Theorie und Praxis in der Lehrerinnen- und Lehrerausbildung. Berlin: Verlag für Wissenschaft und Kultur

Meyer, H. (2004): Was ist guter Unterricht? Berlin: Cornelsen Scriptor

Meyer, H.-D. (2009): Institutionelle Isomorphie und Vielfalt. Zu einer überfälligen Korrektur in der Bildungsforschung. In: Koch, S.; Schemman, M. (eds.): Neo-Institutionalismus in der Erziehungswissenschaft. Wiesbaden: Verlag für Sozialwissenschaften, 292–308

Meyer, R. (2000): Qualifizierung für moderne Beruflichkeit. Münster, New York, München, Berlin: Waxmann

Meyer-Drawe, K. (2000): Illusionen von Autonomie. Diesseits von Ohnmacht und Allmacht des Ich. München: E. Krichheim

Meyer-Drawe, K. (2007): 'Du sollst dir kein Bildnis noch Gleichnis machen ...' – Bildung und Versagung. In: Koller, H.-C.; Marotzki, W.; Sanders, O. (eds.): Bildungsprozesse und Fremdheitserfahrung. Bielefeld: Transcript, 83–94

Meyer-Drawe, K. (2008): Diskurse des Lernens. München: Fink

Meyer-Guckel, V. (2014): Form folgt Funktion: Wie neue Organisationseinheiten für Forschung und Lehre jenseits der Fakultäten die Hochschulen verändern. In: Krempkow, R.; Lottmann, A.; Möller, T. (eds.) (2014): Völlig losgelöst? Governance der Wissenschaft. Band der 6. iFQ-Jahrestagung. Working Paper No. 15. Berlin: Institut für Forschungsinformation und Qualitätssicherung. [See: www.forschungsinfo.de/Publikationen/Download/working_paper_15_2014.pdf, latest access: 10.03.2015], 27–36

Morrow, V.; Richards, M. (1996): The Ethics of Social Research with Children an Overview. In: Children and Society 10, 90–105

Müller-Fohrbrodt, G.; Cloetta, B.; Dann, H.D. (1978): Der Praxisschock bei jungen Lehrern. Stuttgart: Klett

Neuweg, H.G. (2005): Wie grau ist alle Theorie, wie grün des Lebens goldner Baum? LehrerInnenbildung im Spannungsfeld von Theorie und Praxis. In: ÖFEB Newsletter 5 (1), 5–15

Neuweg, H.G. (2010): Fortbildung im Kontext eines phasenübergreifenden Gesamtkonzepts der Lehrerbildung. In: Müller, F.H.; Eichenberger, A.; Lüders, M.; Mayr, J. (eds.): Lehrerinnen und Lehrer lernen. Konzepte und Befunde zur Lehrerfortbildung. Münster, New York, München, Berlin: Waxmann, 35–50

Nölle, K. (2004): Wissensaufbau unterrichtsrelevanten pädagogischen Wissens in der universitären Lehrerbildung. Gesamtergebnisse einer vergleichenden Evaluationsstudie. Referat: Bildung über die Lebenszeit. Internationaler Kongress an der Universität Zürich. Siehe: http://www.paed-kongress04.unizh.ch/veranstaltungen/lehrerbildung/slb2.html

Nohl, H. (1997): Die pädagogische Bewegung in Deutschland und ihre Theorie. Frankfurt/Main: Verlag Schulte-Bulmke

Oelkers, J. (1991): Topoi der Sorge. Beobachtungen zur öffentlichen Verwendung pädagogischen Wissens. In: Oelkers, J.; Tenorth, H.-E. (eds.): Pädagogisches Wissen. Beiheft 27 der Zeitschrift für Pädagogik. Weinheim, Basel: Beltz

Oelkers, J. (2007): Heile Welt und Kinderstube. Performanzen der Erziehung im 19. Jahrhundert. In: Wulf, Ch.; Zirfas, J. (eds.): Pädagogik des Performativen. Theorien, Methoden, Perspektiven. Weinheim, Basel: Beltz, 124–136

Oelkers, J.; Oser, F. (eds.) (2001): Die Wirksamkeit der Lehrerbildungssysteme. Von der Allrounder-Ausbildung zur Ausbildung professioneller Standards. Zürich: Rüegger

Oevermann, U. (2000). Die Methode der Fallrekonstruktion in der Grundlagenforschung sowie der klinischen und pädagogischen Praxis. In: Kraimer, K. (ed.): *Die Fallrekonstruktion. Sinnverstehen in der sozialwissenschaftlichen Forschung.* Frankfurt/Main: Suhrkamp

Oevermann, U. (2001): Die Struktur sozialer Deutungsmuster. Versuch einer Aktualisierung. In: Sozialer Sinn, 1/01, 35–81

Organization for Economic Cooperative Development OECD (2001): Definition and Selection of Competencies: Theoretical and Concetual Foundations (DeSeCo): Background Paper. Paris, FR. Available at: http://www.oecd.org/pisa/35070367.pdf

Oser, F. (1997a): Standards in der Lehrerbildung. Teil 1: Berufliche Kompetenzen, die hohen Qualitätsmerkmalen entsprechen. In: Beiträge zur Lehrerbildung, 15/1, 26–37

Oser, F. (1997b): Standards in der Lehrerbildung. Teil 2: Wie werden Standards in der Schweizerischen Lehrerbildung erworben? Erste empirische Ergebnisse. In: Beiträge zur Lehrerbildung, 15/1, 210–228

Peirce, C.S. ([1903] 1934): Pragmatism and Pragmaticism. Vol. V. Book I Lectures on Pragmatism [held at Harvard University]. Cambridge/Mass.: Harvard University Press

Petersen, S. (2001): Rituale für kooperatives Lernen in der Grundschule. Berlin

Peterßen, W.H. (1996): Lehrbuch Allgemeine Didaktik, München: Ehrenwirth

Plessner, A. ([1970] 1980): Anthropologie der Sinne. In: Gesammelte Schriften in zehn Bänden. Vol. III. Frankfurt/Main: Suhrkamp

Polanyi, M. (1962): Personal Knowledge: Towards a Post-Critical Philosophy. Chicago, London: The University of Chicago Press

Polanyi, M. (1966): The Tacit Dimension. Garden City, New York: Doubleday

Polanyi, M. (1969): Knowing and Being. London, New York: Routledge

Popper, K.R. (1969): Conjectures and Refutations. The Growth of Scientific Knowledge. London, New York: Routledge

Popper, K.R. (1979): Objective Knowledge: An Evolutionary Approach. Oxford: Oxford University Press

Popper, K.R. (1992): The Logic of Scientific Discovery. London, New York: Routledge

Prengel, A. (1993): Kulturen der Vielfalt. Verschiedenheit und Gleichberechtigung in interkultureller, feministischer und integrativer Pädagogik. Opladen: Leske & Budrich

Priority program (SPP) 1293 of the DFG, Available: http://kompetenzmodelle.dipf.de/de [latest access: 10.03.2015]

Reckwitz, A. (2003): Grundelemente einer Theorie sozialer Praktiken. Eine sozialtheoretische Perspektive. In: Zeitschrift für Soziologie 32/4, 282–301

Rhein, R. (2010): Lehrkompetenz und wissenschaftsbezogene Reflexion. In: Zeitschrift für Hochschulentwicklung 5/3, 29–56

Rheinberger, H.J. (2006): Epistemologie des Konkreten. Studien zur Geschichte der modernen Biologie. Frankfurt/Main: Suhrkamp

Röbe, E. (2014): Auf die Haltung kommt es an. Überlegungen zu einer Dimension pädagogischen Denkens und Handelns. Unpublished Paper.

Rolff, H.G.; Zimmermann P. (1993): Kindheit im Wandel. Eine Einführung in die Sozialisation im Kindesalter. Weinheim, Basel: Beltz

Rouse, J. (1999): Understanding Scientific Practices: Cultural Studies of Science as a Philosophical Program. In: Biagioli, M. (ed.): Science Studies Reader. London, New York: Routledge, 442–56

Ryle, G. ([1949] 1963): The Concept of Mind. Chicago, London: The University of Chicago Press

Saldern, M. von (2010): Systemische Schulentwicklung. Von der Grundlegung zur Innovation. Norderstedt: Books on Demand

Schatzki, T.R. (1996): Social Practices. A Wittgensteinian Approach to Human Activity and the Social. Cambridge: University Press

Scheiring, H. (1998): Subjektive Theorien von Schülern über aggressives Handeln. Anwendung eines Dialog-Konsens-Verfahrens bei Hauptschülern. Weinheim: Deutscher Studienverlag

Schleiermacher, F. (1957): Pädagogische Schriften. Die Vorlesungen aus dem Jahre 1826. Vol. I. Düsseldorf, München: Verlag Helmut Küpper

Schnädelbach, H. (1983): Philosophie in Deutschland 1831–1933. Frankfurt/Main: Suhrkamp

Schön, D.A. (1983): The Reflexive Practitioner. How Practitioners Think in Action. New York: Basic Books

Schott, F.; Ghanbari, S.A. (2008): Kompetenzdiagnostik, Kompetenzmodelle, kompetenzorientierter Unterricht. Zur Theorie und Praxis überprüfbarer Bildungsstandards. Münster, New York, München, Berlin: Waxmann

Schröttner, B.T. (2010): The effects of globalization phenomena on educational concepts. In: US-China Education Review, Volume 7, No. 8 (Serial No. 69). Available: http://files.eric.ed.gov/fulltext/ED514734.pdf [15.03.2015]

Schütz, A. (1945): On Multiple Realities. In: Philosophy and Phenomenological Research 5/4, 533–576

Secretary of the Standing Conference of the State Ministers of Education and the Arts in the Federal Republic of Germany KMK (2004): Standards für die Lehrerbildung: Bericht der Arbeitsgruppe. Available: http://www.kmk.org/fileadmin/veroeffentlichungen_beschluesse/2004/2004_12_16-Standards_Lehrerbildung-Bericht_der_AG.pdf [latest access: 10.03.2015]

Setton, D. (2006): Unvermögen – Akrasia – Infantia. Zur problematischen Struktur rationaler Vermögen (unpublished doctoral thesis)

Skolverket (2009): Vad påverkar resultaten i svensk grundskola? Kunskapsöversikt om betydelsen av olika faktorer. Stockholm: Ordförrådet AB

Smith, J.P.; di Sessa, A.; Roschelle, J. (1993): Misconceptions Reconceived: A Constructivist Analysis of Knowledge in Transition. In: Journal of the Learning Sciences 3, 115–163

Stadelmann, M. (2006): Differenz oder Vermittlung? Zum Verhältnis von Theorie und Praxis im Urteil von Praktikumslehrpersonen der Primar- und Sekundarstufe I. Bern, Zürich: Hep-Verlag

Steiner, E. (2004): Erkenntnisentwicklung durch Arbeiten am Fall. Ein Beitrag zur Theorie fallbezogenen Lehrens und Lernens in Professionsausbildungen mit besonderer Berücksichtigung des Semiotischen Pragmatismus von Charles Sanders Peirce. Zürich: University Zürich, Doctoral Dissertation 2004. Available at: http://www.tu-berlin.de/fileadmin/i49/dokumente/1143711480_diss_steiner.pdf

Stelzer-Rothe, G. (2005): Kompetenzen in der Hochschullehre. Rüstzeug für gutes Lehren und Lernen an Hochschulen. Rinteln: Merkur Verlag

Stojanov, K. (2004): Bildung und Anerkennung. Ein intersubjektivitätstheoretischer Ansatz zum pädagogischen Handeln und Bedingungen soziokultureller Pluralität. Univ. Magdeburg, Habilitationsschrift

Tenorth, E. (1989): Deutsche Erziehungswissenschaft im frühen 20.Jahrhundert. In: Zedler, P.; König, E. (eds.): Rekonstruktionen pädagogischer Wissenschaftsgeschichte. Fallstudien, Ansätze, Perspektiven. Weinheim: Deutscher Studien Verlag, 117–140

Tenorth, E. (2006): Professionalität im Lehrerberuf. Ratlosigkeit der Theorie, gelingende Praxis. ZfE 9/4, 580–597

Terhart, E. (2002): Standards für die Lehrer(innen)bildung. Eine Expertise für die Kultusministerkonferenz. Universität Münster: Zentrale Koordination Lehrer(innen)bildung. ZKL-Texte Nr. 24. Münster

Terhart, E. (2007): Universität und Lehrerbildung: Perspektiven einer Partnerschaft. In: Casale, R.; Horlacher, R. (eds.): Bildung und Öffentlichkeit. Jürgen Oelkers zum 60. Geburtstag. Weinheim; Basel: Beltz, 203–219

Terhart, E.; Czerwenka, E.; Ehrich, K.; Jordan, F.; Schmidt, H.J. (1994): Bildungsbiographien von Lehrern und Lehrerinnen. Frankfurt/Main, Berlin, Bern, Wien: Lang

The Board of the German Association of Educational Research DGfE (ed.) (2001): Empfehlungen für ein Kerncurriculum Erziehungswissenschaft. Available at: http://www.dgfe.de/fileadmin/OrdnerRedakteure/Stellungnahmen/2001_KC_EW.pdf [latest access: 10.03.2015]

The Board of the German Association of Educational Research DGfE (ed.) (2004): Kerncurriculum für das Hauptfachstudium Erziehungswissenschaft. Available at: http://www.dgfe.de/fileadmin/OrdnerRedakteure/Stellungnahmen/2004_01_KC_HF_EW.pdf [latest access: 10.03.2015]

The Board of the German Association of Educational Research DGfE (ed.) (2005): Strukturmodell für die Lehrerbildung im Bachelor/Bakkalaureus- und Master/Magister-System. Available at: http://www.dgfe.de/fileadmin/OrdnerRedakteure/Stellungnahmen/2005_Strukturmodell_BA_MA_Lehramt.pdf [latest access: 10.03.2015]

Tillmann, K.-J. (2006): Systemsteuerung durch Leistungsvergleiche und Bildungsstandards? Oder: Kritische Anmerkungen zum gegenwärtigen Zeitgeist. In: Heinrich, M.; Greiner, U. (eds.): Schauen, was 'rauskommt. Kompetenzförderung, Evaluation und Systemsteuerung im Bildungswesen. Wien: LIT-Verlag, 13–35

Trowler, P.; Bamber, R. (2005): Compulsory Higher Education Teacher Training: Joined-up policies, institutional architectures and enhancement cultures. In: International Journal for Academic Development 10/2, Nov. 2005, 79–93

Ulich, K. (1996): Lehrer/innen-Ausbildung im Urteil der Betroffenen. Ergebnisse und Folgerungen. In: Die Deutsche Schule 88, H.1, 81–97

Vogel, P. (1998): Vorschlag für ein Modell erziehungswissenschaftlicher Wissensformen. In: Borrelli, M.; Ruhloff, J. (eds.): Interdisziplinäre Verflechtungen und interdisziplinäre Differenzierungen. Hohengehren, Baltmannsweiler: Schneider Verlag, 173–185

Wacker, A.; Maier, U.; Wissinger, J. (2012): Schul- und Unterrichtsreform durch ergebnisorientierte Steuerung. Empirische Befunde und forschungsmethodische Implikationen – Educational Governance 9. Wiesbaden: Springer VS

Wagner-Willi, M. (2004): Videointerpretation als mehrdimensionale Mikroanalyse am Beispiel schulischer Alltagsszenen. In: Zeitschrift für Qualitative Bildungs-, Beratungs- und Sozialforschung 1, 49–66

Wahl, D. (1991): Handeln unter Druck. Weinheim: Deutscher Studienverlag

Waldenfels, B. (1990): Der Stachel des Fremden. Frankfurt/Main: Suhrkamp

Waldenfels, B. (1992): Einführung in die Phänomenologie. München

Waldenfels, B. (1994): Antwortregister. Frankfurt/Main: Suhrkamp

Waldenfels, B. (1998): Grenzen der Normalisierung. Studien zur Phänomenologie des Fremden 2. Frankfurt/Main: Suhrkamp

Waldenfels, B. (2000): Das leibliche Selbst. Frankfurt/Main: Suhrkamp

Waldenfels, B. (2004a): Phänomenologie der Aufmerksamkeit. Frankfurt/Main: Suhrkamp

Waldenfels, B. (2004b): Findigkeit des Körpers. Dortmund: Dortmunder Schriften zur Kunst

Waldow, F. (2014): From Taylor to Tyler to *No Child Left Behind*: Legitimating educational standards. In: Droux, J.; Hofstetter, R. (eds.): Les savoirs dans le champ éducatif: Circulations, transformations, implementations: Pour une histoire sociale de la fabrique internationale des savoirs en éducation 19e-20e siècles. Rennes: PUR

Walters, J.; Gardner, H. (1986): The crystallizing experience: Discovering an intellectual gift. In: Sternberg, R.J.; Davidson, J.E. (eds.): Conceptions of giftedness. Cambridge: Cambridge University Press, 306–331

Weber, A. (2005): Problem-Based Learning – Ansatz zur Verknüpfung von Theorie und Praxis. In: Beiträge zur Lehrerbildung 23(1), 94–104

Weinert, F.E. (2001): Concept of Competence: a Conceptual Clarification. In: Rychen, D.S.; Salganik, L.H. (eds.): Defining and Selecting Key Competencies. Seattle: Hogrefe & Huber Publishers, 45–65

Weingardt, M. (2004): Fehler zeichnen uns aus. Transdisziplinäre Grundlagen zur Theorie und Produktivität des Fehlers in Schule und Arbeitswelt. Bad Heilbrunn: Klinkhardt

Weniger, E. ([1929] 1975): Theorie und Praxis in der Erziehung. In: Weniger, E.: Ausgewählte Schriften zur geisteswissenschaftlichen Pädagogik. Weinheim, Basel: Beltz, 29–44

Westphal, K. (2004): Lernen als Ereignis – Zugänge zu einem theaterpädagogischen Projekt. Baltmannsweiler: Schneider Verlag Hohengehren

Winkel, R. (1988): Antinomische Pädagogik und Kommunikative Didaktik. Studien zu den Widersprüchen und Spannungen in Erziehung und Schule. Düsseldorf: Schwann-Bagel

Winkler, M. (2006): Bildung mag zwar die Antwort sein – das Problem aber ist die Erziehung. In: Zeitschrift fü Sozialpädgogik 4 (2), 182–201

Wirth, U. (2001): Abduktion als Spiel. In: Zeitschrift für Semiotik 23 (3–4), 379–392

Wittenbruch, W. (1995): Grundschule. Texte und Bilder zur Geschichte einer jungen Schulstufe. Heinsberg: Dieck

Wittenbruch, W. (2010): Theorien des Unterrichts. In: Hellekamps, S.; Plöger, W.; Wittenbruch, W. (eds.): Schule, Handbuch der Erziehungswissenschaft 3, Studienausgabe. Paderborn, Münster, Wien, Zürich: Ferdinand Schöningh, 231–249

Wulf, Ch. (1997): Vom Menschen – Handbuch Historische Anthropologie. Weinheim, Basel: Beltz

Wulf, Ch.; Zirfas, J. (2004): Die Kultur des Rituals. Inszenierungen, Praktiken, Symbole. München: Wilhelm Fink

Wulf, Ch.; Zirfas, J. (2007): Performative Pädagogik und performative Bildungstheorien. Ein neuer Fokus erziehungswissenschaftlicher Forschung. In: Wulf, Ch.; Zirfas, J. (eds.): Pädagogik des Performativen. Theorien, Methoden, Perspektiven. Weinheim, Basel: Beltz, 7–40

Wulff, H.J. (1998): Störmanöver. In: Fischer-Lichte, E.; Kolesch D. (eds.): Paragrana. Internationale Zeitschrift für Historische Anthropologie 7 (1): Kulturen des Performativen, 215–220

Zeiher, H. (2001): Children's Islands in Space and Time. The Impact of Spatial Differentiation on Children's Ways of Shaping Social Life. In: du Bois-Reymond, M.;

Suenker, H.; Krueger, H.-H. (eds.): Childhood in Europe: Approaches – Trends – Findings. New York: Peter Lang, 139–159

Zinnecker, J. (1975): Der heimliche Lehrplan. Untersuchungen zum Schulunterricht. Weinheim, Basel: Beltz

Zinnecker, J. (1978): Die Schule als Hinterbühne oder Nachrichten aus dem Unterleben der Schüler. In: Reinert, B.; Zinnecker, J. (eds.): Schüler im Schulbetrieb. Berichte und Bilder vom Lernalltag, von Lernpausen und vom Lernen in den Pausen. Reinbek bei Hamburg, 29–121

Zirfas, J. (1999): Bildung als Entbildung. In: Schäfer, G.; Wulf, Ch. (eds.): Bild – Bilder – Bildung. Weinheim: Deutscher Studienverlag, 159–194

Zirfas, J. (2001): Identitäten und Dekonstruktionen. Pädagogische Überlegungen in Anschluss an Jacques Derrida. In: Fritzsche, B.; Schmidt, A.; Hartmann, J. (eds.): Dekonstruktive Pädagogik. Erziehungswissenschaftliche Debatten unter poststrukturalistischen Perspektiven. Opladen: Leske & Budrich, 49–64

Zirfas, J. (2010): Jacques Derrida: Das andere Kap. Die vertagte Demokratie. Zwei Essays zu Europa. In: Jörissen, B.; Zirfas, J. (eds.): Schlüsselwerke der Pädagogik. Wiesbaden: Verlag für Sozialwissenschaften, 241–258

European Studies on Educational Practices

Bosse Bergstedt, Anna Herbert,
Anja Kraus, Christoph Wulf (ed.)

Tacit Dimensions of Pedagogy

2012, 136 pages, pb, € 24,90,
ISBN 978-3-8309-2649-8
E-Book: € 21,99,
ISBN 978-3-8309-7649-3

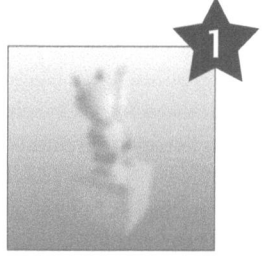

Looking at educational practices is not reduced to the explicit decisions concerning aims, subjects and schedules. It also entails the examination of the inexplicable knowledge on which social relations are based. Sensual perceptions and time-space-object relations are important frames of the practical orientation and influences of non-formal learning on formal learning situations are explored.

Bosse Bergstedt, Anna Herbert,
Anja Kraus (ed.)

Initiating Learning

2012, 156 pages, pb, € 24,90
ISBN 978-3-8309-2650-4
E-Book: € 21,99,
ISBN 978-3-8309-7650-9

Learning is carried out by implicit attitudes and is influenced by opaque actual happenings such as subtexts of a spoken text, forms of bodily communication and interaction and by the material conditions of learning processes and their limitations. The endeavour to initiate learning cannot but deal with its explicit as well as with its tacit aspects.

Anna Herbert, Anja Kraus (ed.)

Praxeology as a Challenge

Modelling the Tacit Dimensions of Pedagogy

2013, 128 pages, pb, € 24,90,
ISBN 978-3-8309-2651-1
E-Book: € 21,99,
ISBN 978-3-8309-7651-6

The empirical question how social practices constitute a (binding) reality comes close to the praxeological perspective. All the mainly empirical studies in this volume deal with the praxeological question how sociality is generated in dynamic and relational actions in a pedagogical frame.

Anja Kraus, Mie Buhl,
Gerd-Bodo von Carlsburg (ed.)

Performativity, Materiality and Time

Tacit Dimensions of Pedagogy

2014, 152 pages, pb, € 24,90,
ISBN 978-3-8309-3116-4
E-Book: € 21,99,
ISBN 978-3-8309-8116-9

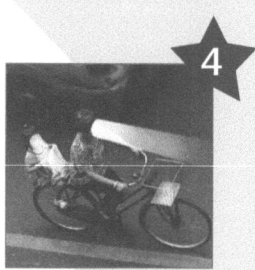

Focusing mainly on the tacit side of pedagogical practices entails not only a revision of instructional practices but also of the theoretical approaches to educational practices and a work on the methodology of empirical research in the Educational Sciences. In terms of this effort references to subjects, objects and given structures are replaced by the concepts performativity, materiality and time.

WAXMANN
www.waxmann.com
info@waxmann.com